THE

MORMONS AT HOME;

With some Incidents of Travel

FROM

MISSOURI TO CALIFORNIA,

1852-3.

IN A SERIES OF LETTERS.

BY MRS. B. G. FERRIS,

~~~~~~~~~

AMS PRESS
NEW YORK

Reprinted from the edition of 1856, New York
First AMS edition Published 1971

Manufactured in the United States of America

International Standard Book Number: 0-404-08437-0

Library of Congress Catalog Card Number: 70-134395

AMS PRESS INC.
NEW YORK, N. Y. 10003

PREFACE.

In the summer of 1852 my husband received from the President an appointment for the territory of Utah, which he was induced to accept. Unwilling to be separated from him, for the length of time he must necessarily be absent, under circumstances involving much anxiety for his safety, I determined to accompany him. We accordingly journeyed to Salt Lake, where we spent the winter; and, in the succeeding spring, returned home by way of California.

During our absence, and in compliance with a previous promise, I wrote letters to some near and dear friends, descriptive of our travel and sojourn in Utah. Since our return, I have collected and revised these letters, as a matter of amusement. Those relating to the journey were written with more or less haste, and under the usual inconveniences of camp life; I have studied, however, to preserve the passing impressions and reflections, as they actually occurred. In Utah I could not well avoid some intercourse with its female society; and became, necessarily, conversant with the effect upon it of the more distinctive features of Mormonism.

Yielding to the suggestion, that these incidents of travel and impressions of Mormonism may be interesting to the public, I have, with some hesitation, given my letters to the publishers.

ITHACA, N. Y., Dec., 1855.

CONTENTS.

LETTER XVI.

LETTER I.

INDEPENDENCE, Mo., Aug. 20th, 1852.

BIDDING adieu to our kind friends in St. Louis on the 12th, we have since been steaming up that mighty arm of western commerce—the Missouri. Just for a moment step on board, in imagination, and gain a bird's eye view of this inland voyage. The brave vessel boldly turns her figure-head into the mouth of this rushing, muddy, turbid highway of waters, and crushes through its chevaux-de-frise of snags, or glides softly over them— feeling her way along, as if uncertain which side is the safe one—anon retracing her steps for another current, and performing all sorts of evolutions to avoid hidden . dangers—and sometimes, in spite of the pilot's skill, coming to a dead halt, with one wheel actually

1

grappling with the treacherous saurians and river gods, which lurk in the muddy bottom.

On board we have a little world, gathered from all parts of the great world. A nice, motherly German woman, fresh from fatherland, as her high-crowned cap and antique costume indicate, is gazing wistfully upon the shore, while her stalwart son points with hopeful anticipation to the rich soil upon the banks, comparing it with the worn-out lands they have left. But she shakes her head— "*Nein, Nein,*" is her only answer—the gesture and the words express the emotions of her honest soul. The pretty home on the banks of the Rhine—husband, children, friends—all gone but this one son.

As a contrast to this blue-eyed matron, we have a helpless southern lady, with three equally helpless children, who seem to have been born into the world for the mere business of crying and vexation. This inert specimen of womanhood is soft and languishing; lounges on the sofa, looking pretty in her light muslins; and exhibits now and then sufficient animation to direct the slave girl to see whether

Johnny wont fall overboard, or what Minnie is crying for. The girl, however, takes the matter very coolly, until a busy-body of an old woman, with a vigorous push, assures her that one child will certainly be overboard in "mighty quick time," unless she sees to it. Was there ever a steamer yet but had some Johnny to persist in using the railing for a hobby horse, to the distress of tender mothers.

Another contrast still, is a noble-looking western woman, a Mrs. K——. After arranging her and her son's state-rooms to her satisfaction—which was only accomplished by sundry threats and a few bribes to the fashionable stewardess—she sailed down through the long saloon to the kitchen (who ever dreamed a steamer had a kitchen?), with her cap strings flying, to see, as she expressively said, whether she could eat in any comfort. Her brow, which had worn rather a threatening aspect, was smoothed on her return. The report was favorable—the floor was white—the table neat —and, above all, she said, the stew pans were clean, really clean, and hung up, just as her cook Sally kept hers. We laughed one and all. She said if we had seen what she had, in these Missouri steamer kitchens, we would never want to eat again—which would be no laughing matter.

Next to our state-room is an East India woman, with a babe and consumptive husband. He is an Englishman by birth, but has always lived in Hindostan, and is now in search of health and a brother. To-day they are to land on the northern side of the river. She is intelligent and communicative, and has the black hair, olive complexion, brilliant eyes, and peculiar ornaments of one from eastern lands.

We have, also, a little, tidy maiden lady, who is devoting her life to the difficult task of converting the Indians to her own faith. She has already been two years at the Shawnee mission, and her soul seems to be in the business, if we are to judge from the incessant stream of uninteresting incidents of the half civilized nations, which she pours forth without mercy.

Among the rarer curiosities of our floating human menagerie is a most forlorn-looking couple—man and woman—on the lower deck.

Each day they are to be seen sitting at the extreme end of the boat, without the least shelter from the burning sun. The woman has no covering but a thin cotton dress. There she sits, day after day, gazing listlessly into the water, and showing no signs of life, except to toss back her long, black tresses of uncombed hair. The man is evidently much older than she, and guards her with zealous care, his arm around her, as though to keep her from plunging into the turbid waters. Who are they? Has she been rescued by her father or brother from some den of infamy in St. Louis? Or are they mere clods—merely one of nature's specimens of stupidity?

Our little saloon gradually threw off all reserve, and were as social and familiar as friends of longers tanding; so much so, that Mrs. K. and her husband urged me to stay with them at Liberty, while the further preparations for our journey were going on at Independence.

On Monday we landed at Fort Wayne— everything is a *fort* here—and, as the steamer moved off to pursue her voyage, it seemed as though the last link connecting us with civilized life had been broken. While waiting at a building which was called a hotel, probably by way of joke, for a carriage to convey us to Independence, we were favored with a specimen of the western "chills," the kind which the landlady assured us never left the patient till he "shook them out." The poor man looked as though he might shake himself out at the same time. Everything was hot, humid, and uncomfortable. The ride to Independence made some amends for this chilly reception. It is a sunny region, with beautiful glens, and magnificent oaks and elms, and everything green and luxuriant.

At present we are domesticated at the Nebraska House, externally of great pretensions, but the host has "a mighty hard time to carry it on," as they say here. When he turns his back there is a species of "high life below stairs" going on, which produces a perfect Babel of sounds. The performances, however, at the table, are ludicrous enough. The head waiter has a world of trouble with his sable assistants, and frequently throws down his napkin and dignity together, and starts in full pursuit when they fail to take off the covers exactly at the signal. His wrath, however, is more laughably spent on two young blacks, whose duty it is to keep in motion some queer machinery over the table, to prevent our devouring more flies than the cook has served up. The result is, that we are favored with a regular *chassez* to the right and left: the young sables, however, make up in agility what they lack in strength, and manage to escape by diving under the table on one side, to reappear on the other. But, notwithstanding these drill exercises, there is such unmistakable kindness, and so liberal a supply of substantials and luxuries, that we enjoy it very well.

The ladies of the house I see flitting about in their white muslins, looking as disengaged and unconcerned as visitors. The old cook is evidently at the head of the establishment, and, under her benign reign, the pigs and chickens struggle for the freedom of the kitchen with the darkies, though I do not think they actually gain an entrance.

The town is pleasantly situated, the scenery around, judging from our ride from the river, possessing beauty, with few, if any, features of boldness. It was originally selected as the seat of Mormon power; and a beautiful site for their temple is pointed out, now occupied by a pretty cottage, with tastefully arranged grounds. It is a frontier town, where emigrant parties fit out for the plains; huge covered wagons are standing in different places, some new and others dismantled; immense ox teams pass by, and mules are common. Opposite our room they are branding the mules for our caravan, a business attended with rough usage and unnecessary cruelty.

LETTER II.

START FROM INDEPENDENCE——A BREAK-DOWN ——WESTPORT——DESCRIPTION OF THE TRAIN—— INDIANS——OUR FIRST CAMP.

SHAWNEE COUNTRY, eight miles from Westport,
Aug. 25, 1852.

BEHOLD us at the first stage of our far western journey ! We left Independence day before
yesterday, with as much delight as children
setting forth on a holiday excursion, though I
hope not quite so thoughtless, in reference to
future contingencies.

These border Missourians are more hospitable than neat; and we had been detained so
long in procuring mules, and other things
necessary for the expedition, and had so tired
of living at a public-house, that we became
quite anxious to exchange its numberless disagreeables for life upon " the Plains." Of course
we got under weigh, after so long a prepara-

1*

tion, with some little eclat—two darkies at the head of our leaders to keep them in the right direction, and prevent them from doubling around, and running into the carriage—our host in attendance, at the head of the usual loungers at a hotel, to whom was added a reinforcement from the street—our driver gave a few extra cracks of his whip, and, under the echo of a hearty good-by, away we went, almost at top speed.

Our mules possess the usual eccentricities of the race, but, to say truth, behaved remarkably well during the first drive, except that now and then the leaders would most obstinately turn out to crop the grass by the way-side. On we went, gaily enough, and were congratulating ourselves how well we were getting along, when, going up a sharp, rocky pitch, within a mile of Westport, the lead chain gave way, and our wheel mules, from the entire load being suddenly thrown upon them, were in a fair way of being dragged over a steep bank. Our situation, for a few moments, was critical enough; but, fortunately, a mule has, at least, the virtue of never

willingly going backwards for "love or whip:"
In this instance they struggled hard against
the pressure, and we were soon extricated
from our disagreeable predicament.

This mishap involved the momentous consequence of spending another night within the
bounds of civilization, "so-called," instead of
"camping out" in the Indian country. Un-
luckily, the hotel had been burned down within
a few days, and we were compelled to seek
refuge in a private boarding-house; and I
shall not soon forget the low, hot, ill-ven-
tilated room, nor the cotillions danced on our
bed by a lively party of mice. I think Punch
must have fiddled for them; for, between
snatches of sleeping and waking, I heard all
sorts of sounds. Our hostess, however, was
kind-hearted, and gave me some Indian words,
by which I could repulse the squaws in case
of their becoming too intrusive.

The next morning the broken chain was
duly mended, and, about noon, we were joined
by the rest of the party, and set forth in
good earnest on our great journey. We have
thirteen men, all well armed. It is a mer-

chant's train, with four large wagons contain-
ing goods for the Salt Lake market, each
drawn by six mules, and each has a rifle
strapped on its side by way, I suppose, of
making a formidable show.   Then there is
Capt. Phelps, who is our commander and
guide, with his wife and child; and they are
drawn by four mules in a very commodious
carriage.   Then our humble selves in another
carriage, and a small baggage-wagon to bring
up the rear.   Our carriage has fairly become
our domicil—our parlor, kitchen, and bed-
room—and you would be perfectly astonished
at the quantity of goods and chattels which
we have been able to stow in and around it,
for the necessities and conveniences of the
journey:—blankets, buffalo-robe, shawls, um-
brella, overcoat, port-folio, books, basket, car-
pet-bag, ham, pickles, pistols, and other things
"too numerous to mention."   And then we
have, underneath, jingling and rattling, camp-
kettles, frying-pans, etc.   If we are not mistaken for peddlers, it will not be for want
of all the regular symptoms.   Our train, when
stretched out in the road, with its accom-

paniment of spare mules, looked quite imposing; but I could not quite shut out my
womanly anticipation, that it would be diminutive enough, surrounded, in hostile fashion, by five hundred whooping and shouting
savages. The men, however, say there is no
danger, and I have hopefully made up my
mind to believe them.

About a mile from Westport we crossed
the extreme western bounds of Missouri, and
fairly launched on our untried adventures.
The ride was perfectly delightful; and, if this
is a fair sample of the road over the much-
talked of "Plains," it will be more like a
pleasure excursion than a wearisome journey.
The country was beautiful—slightly undulating, with patches of fine open woods—and
here and there a cultivated field of some Indian
or white borderer.

We met numbers of the natives riding towards Westport, on small, wild-looking ponies,
some of whom were decorated in the extreme
of Indian dandyism. One girl careered along
unembarrassed by side-saddle or skirt, but
very much dressed:—a pink apron flounced

all the way up, red leggins fringed and tas-
seled, beautiful moccasins, an abundance of
tinsel ornaments jingling about her ears and
neck, a gay shawl tied carelessly over one
shoulder, a bead-work sash around her waist,
and a pretty handkerchief around her head,
from which fluttered a red streamer in the
wind. She undoubtedly thought herself an
object of envy by us poor, plain mortals. And
then she rode with such a careless, yet graceful abandon, that it seemed as though she
had been born, bred, and brought up on the
pony's back.

Some of the squaws looked ugly, and, as
I fancied, expressed much malignity in their
glances towards us. We passed a party of
about a dozen Caw chiefs and dignitaries on
a visit to the Shawnees. They were under
a small but beautiful clump of trees by the
way-side, had scalp tufts and scarlet blankets, some nearly but not quite in the condition of model artists, some stretched on the
grass, others leaning on their rifles, and others,
again, against the trees in attitudes of careless dignity. I have seldom looked upon a

more picturesque scene. They did not appear
to notice us, but scanned our animals with
great apparent attention.

We reached our first camp-ground about
six, P. M., near a fine spring, on ground slightly
rolling. Our mules were soon unharnessed,
and allowed to crop the luxuriant grass with
long ropes dragging from their necks. At
night they were caught by these ropes, and
fastened to picket-pins driven into the ground,
and thus afforded a circle of a diameter twice
the length of the rope, within which to finish
their evening meal. On our left, and just
beyond a slight hollow, are two Indian huts,
and some half a dozen of both sexes, and of
rather forbidding appearance, made themselves
spectators of our camping operations, occasionally taking a drink from a bottle, and
laughing in very harsh tones.

The camp arranged itself into three messes,
our own consisting of Denton, Morse, and ourselves, and a corresponding number of fires
were built upon the ground. Denton came
with us from home, and you know something
of him already. Morse is an Illinoian whom

we picked up at St. Louis. It seems he joined a company last spring, for California, at St. Joseph's; was taken sick of the small-pox three miles out from that place, abandoned by his companions, and came near ending his travels an outcast in the woods. A friendly doctor, however, found him out and acted the part of the good Samaritan, and after his convalescence he made his way to St. Louis, where he contrived to scrape together forty dollars, which he paid for his passage in one of the multitude of California companies having their origin in that city. The company broke up, the man to whom he paid his money proved to be a cheat, and we found him completely stranded by the waves of adverse fortune, and ready enough to engage in our service. He is badly marked with small-pox, but his countenance indicates great good nature, with some tendency to sly humor; and, as he at one time served a half-way apprenticeship to a baker, he is likely to prove a valuable acquisition in the preparation of our meals.

To return from this digression, our supper was prepared in a very primitive fashion. As

it was our first essay at camp life, we contented ourselves with a limited variety—ham,
pilot-bread, and coffee—but we enjoyed it with
much zest—and, strange as you may think it,
it was perfectly clean. The shades of evening
came on, the camp fires flickered in the dark,
the men, dressed in red and blue shirts, glided
about, and finally stretched themselves carelessly upon the grass, a company of Indian
ponies galloped about us, and kept neighing
with a peculiar shrillness. Altogether it was
a scene of surpassing strangeness, and I could
not, if I would, describe the mingled sensations of fear and pleasure, which kept me
effectually awake until after midnight. The
night passed over with no other incident than
Mr. F. thrusting his head from the carriage,
and asking the sentinel, whom he mistook for
an Indian, "What are you doing there?" He
had, it seems, thrown a blanket over his shoulders, native fashion, and this morning we have
had plenty of camp witticisms over the mistake. The carriage furnishes a more convenient and roomy sleeping apartment than I
had hoped. The backs of the front and middle

seats are connected with the bottom part by
hinges, and, when unstrapped and turned down,
make a complete, cushioned bed; and, with
the aid of blankets and buffalo robe, we shall
sleep snugly enough.

I slept late, and the first thing I saw on
waking was, the family of our captain cosily
seated on a blanket at breakfast. While our
own was preparing, I could not resist the
temptation of making my first " call." You
can't imagine how relieved I am to find that
I am not the only female of the party. Capt.
Phelps is gentlemanly and very talkative.
Mrs. P. is an exceedingly quiet appearing lady,
and has an infant only four weeks old. I
am determined to like her, and the dear little
baby I have taken to my heart already. In
addition was the driver, who rejoices in the
name of "Doc," and a relative—a tall, gentlemanly man, by the name of Mundy. We are
as much acquainted in five minutes as though
we had known each other all our lives. The
formalities of the drawing-room are here out
of place—it is *"How do you do?"* with a hearty
shake of the hand, *sans ceremonie.*

Our breakfast is a second edition of the supper, with the addition of a sort of johny-cake made of pinola, or ground parched corn. Some of the mules have broken loose, and a couple of Indians are hazing after them, back and forth, on their ponies, at full speed. The men are engaged in harnessing such of the animals as have not escaped, and I cannot help laughing at their vexations. One man is trying to mesmerize a contrary beast, which will neither go backward, nor forward, nor sideways, but stands obstinately braced in every direction. He has whistled to him, and whispered in his ear, and made sundry coaxing passes over his head and neck, but it is of no use. Some one called out, "Why don't you give his ear a thundering twist?" Sure enough that brought the animal to; but it also brought his heels into the air. Why the men don't get killed is to me a wonder.

The captain has concluded to wait here to-day for a few mules to be brought in from Westport, and it is settled that we are to go on to the next camping-ground, some eight miles further.

LETTER III.

PAWNEE COUNTY, Sept. 2, 1852.

HERE we are in the dreaded Pawnee country, and I begin to feel like a veteran traveler. Last evening, after supper, our mules came rushing into camp in the wildest alarm, and some of the men shouted "Indians! Indians!" Mr. F. caught his revolver and jumped from the carriage, and I commenced unfastening a double-barreled gun, knowing that would be the next thing called for. Very soon some one cried—"It is nothing but wolves!" and so, in fact, it proved. But did not I act bravely? By all ordinary rules, I ought to have screamed. I am satisfied that parties traveling over the plains very soon lose all sense of danger. Since the first night spent in camp, I have felt as secure as when at home, with doors and windows fastened. The mules were so prodigiously frightened, that they surrounded the bell pony (the only horse flesh in camp), and so completely worried up the poor thing with their lariats, as to make her lame. You must know that mules look upon horses as superior beings, and will follow them with the same kind of humble submission that a spaniel will his master. Hence it is usual for emigrating parties to have a horse with a bell; and it is said to be often the means of saving the mules from being run off by Indian marauders. Our "bell pony" is a beautiful roan, the property of Mr. Mundy, and withal a general favorite; and it is really gratifying to witness the unremitting care which he bestows upon "Kate."

My first letter left us at our first camping ground, among the Shawnees; and, since then, we have had some vicissitudes by "field," if not by "flood." We started about 11 A. M., in advance of the train, but made only five miles, encamping on the west bank of a small stream, dignified by the name of river; but which, with us, would be termed a creek : the name has escaped me. The other side was thickly wooded for some distance east. The road was fenced on each side, which precluded much choice in selecting our temporary residence; but we found a broad-spreading oak, whose branches afforded some protection from the burning sun. On each side was an Indian log cabin—that on our left very neat in appearance, with a clean yard in front, interspersed with flowers, giving some indications of taste. We soon became acquainted with the inmates, found them friendly, and ready, at reasonable prices, to furnish grain and pasture for our animals. A little back of the hut was an immense field of corn, and they allowed us to select ears for roasting. There were indications of laziness, however, mixed up with this appearance of thrift—two stout-looking men lounged about, laughing and talking with the squaw mother, who stretched herself at full length on the stoop of this "model cottage." The whole establishment would look unthrifty enough in the state of New York, and only attracted attention because it belonged to the natives.

The train came up at evening, but, owing to the escape of some mules, it was understood that we were to go on again in advance.

The next day was one of vexation. Our captain had had his share in the escape of mules—our turn came next. We started very leisurely, and had gone quietly along for about a mile and a half, when we heard a crash, accompanied by a shout from Morse in the rear. The spokes of one of the wheels of the baggage wagon had broken like so many pipe stems, and let that important establishment to the ground. Our commissary department was in a sad fix. Of course we dismounted and walked around the wreck, and held a council of war over the disaster, which resulted in returning to camp, and sending Denton back with the broken wagon for repairs. They all say it takes about a week to get fairly under weigh, and our case was in conformity to the general rule.

The next morning the train left us to go twelve miles—we to follow as soon as Denton returned. As they wound along out of sight, it created a feeling of loneliness not very agreeable. The day was hot, and we found ourselves annoyed by a lot of pigs of all sizes, belonging to our dusky neighbors, who pertinaciously claimed a right to all the odd scraps without waiting our departure.

As soon as we were fairly left alone, two young squaws, with a pappoose, paid me a visit, and brought a fine water-melon. They took a mental inventory of everything inside and out of our traveling wigwam; and, after their return, I could hear them recounting, as I supposed, what they had seen. Of course I could do no less than return this call. They were really friendly. The hut on the left belonged to a chief—Tiger Simon—who was absent. The daughter was a pretty, modest girl—indeed, she might be called beautiful; the mother had the softest and most musical voice I ever heard; the son, who had received some education at the Baptist Mission, acted as interpreter, and we had quite a dish of conversation, in which I learned many particulars of their family history; and this seemed

to please them much. On the other side of
the way they were less neat, but equally
friendly. They were rocking a stout boy,
that I judged to be two years old, in a ham-
mock. I made them understand that I thought
he was too big to rock; they laughed, and
stuck up *one* finger, to signify that he was
only one yèar old. These incidents relieved
the hours somewhat of their tedium.

The day finally wore away; and, as we were
preparing for our supper, a party of about a
dozen Sioux—men, women, and children—rode
by towards Westport with peltry. They had
singular looking whips dangling at the wrist
of the right hand—some of them highly orna-
mented. They eyed us very coolly. The men
were armed with bows and arrows, and looked
something formidable. Two of the old ones
put out their hands and said: "white squaw
give." I shook my head and told them to
begone, with a corresponding gesture; they
persisted a few moments and then went off,
shaking their heads and jabbering to each other
—descanting, probably, on the meanness of
the "white squaw." I begin to think Indian

taciturnity, so much talked of, to be a mere
fiction.

Soon after, a party of ugly-looking Caws,
of about the same number, and of all sizes
and sexes, went by in the other direction.
They eyed us sharply in passing, and, somewhat to my disquiet, camped a short distance
from us. This was a disagreeable addition to
the neighborhood, and I could not help feeling
anxious for the return of Denton. The mules
were some distance off in pasture, and Mr. F.
and Morse went after them, for the purpose of
having them picketed near us, to guard against
a diminution of their numbers among such
suspicious neighbors. During their absence, I,
like a prudent housewife, took a peep into
a kettle of boiling tounque, to see how the
culinary matters were progressing; and, as I
turned around, was confronted by a stout Caw
lad. There he stood, as motionless as a marble
statue; his eyes snaky; a red blanket over
his shoulders; his crown surmounted by the
scalp lock—war fashion. His presence was a
mystery. Had he risen up from the ground,
or fallen down from the clouds? It was at

that period of twilight when objects are apt to assume shapes suited to the fears or fancy of the beholder; I was entirely alone, and the imp probably appeared more imposing than the facts would warrant. I was really startled. I told him to be off; he answered, "I no understand." I then reached into the carriage door, as if for some means of defense, and off strode the rascal, with a tread as measured and stately as Brandt or Tecumseh in the presence of his warriors.

Mr. F. and Morse soon returned; and then a party of Potawatomies came up on the other side of the stream, and lit up the edge of the forest with their camp fire. The scene was, in the last degree, wild and strange, and, to my imagination, somewhat fearful. We were between two camps of savages—literally "between two fires." What if Denton should not come? But the rattling of our mended vehicle soon answered that question quite satisfactorily; and, to crown all, the full moon rose in queenly majesty, and poured a flood of mellow light over the whole.

The night passed off with no other incident

than the loss of a half-eaten ham, but whether stolen by Indians or dogs we took little pains to discover. In the morning our roving neighbors were in motion first, and relieved us of their presence. We soon followed, and, traveling over a rolling prairie, joined our friends in camp near the Wakarusa—a clear, rapid stream.

The country was beautiful. Occasionally a swell of this land-ocean would rise higher than usual, and open to us an extended view, with islands of wood scattered here and there in the distance. The train were preparing supper as we joined them; two of the men had been on an unsuccessful duck hunt, and we were doomed to hear the numberless jokes about crooked guns, weak eyes, etc., which such failures usually elicit. An active-looking Shawnee, however, came in with a supply of prairie chickens and honey, which enabled us to make out a good supper, notwithstanding the failure of our hunters. This man had a fine farm, was very talkative, and said, among other things, that in five years his family would be as good as white folks.

It was Saturday evening, and, as the shades of night thickened around, the memories of home and friends came crowding upon me until I felt wretchedly home-sick.

The next day was the Sabbath, but it gave rest neither to man nor beast. Our captain determined to travel on, to make up the precious time we had lost. We found a beautiful prairie road, which led us about noon over a more elevated point than any we had yet seen. The prospect was extended and magnificent beyond description. The numerous clumps of trees, like orchards, gave the impression of cultivated farms; but we looked in vain for grazing cattle, fences, farm-houses, and fields of grain. We saw, in the distance, to the right, portions of the Kansas, which looked wider than the reality, and resembled small lakes. No living thing was to be seen, except now and then a prairie chicken, and a solitary wolf that cantered off slowly after catching a view of the train.

We descended into a quiet hollow, under a beautiful clump of trees, for dinner; but it was too hot for cooking, and we contented

ourselves with a lunch.   At starting, however,
the mules seemed to think their rights had
been infringed upon, and exhibited their peculiarities in an unusual degree.   It was a dreadful medley of kicks, bites, blows, and curses.
One mule was with difficulty harnessed by five
men; and then, with a single flirt of her heels,
threw every strap and buckle clean from her
body.   After this capital feat, the animal seemed to be perfectly satisfied, and allowed one
man to readjust the harness without difficulty.
They are really comical creatures, and are
often docile enough, after giving a few specimens of ground and lofty tumbling.   We soon
passed from this sequestered spot, which
resumed its quiet and Sabbath-like repose.
The rest of the day's journey brought us to
a fine spring, where we passed a quiet night,
disturbed only by a few plaintive notes from
the prairie wolf, with which we are becoming
acquainted.

The next day's travel was similar to the
last—a succession of rolling prairies, the monotony of which was occasionally relieved by
an elevated point, and an extended and beauti-

ful prospect of hill and valley. The scenery became more diversified and more wooded as we approached the Kansas, which was lined with a beautiful belt of trees. We reached the river in advance of the train, and crossed in a ferry boat in season to encamp on the north bank, anticipating a great deal of trouble with the mules—but, for a wonder, they behaved with commendable propriety. The stream at this point is nearly as broad as the Missouri, and quite as rapid. It was low water; and, after leaving the boat, we crossed a troublesome sand level before reaching the grassy bank. The rest of the train came up, but not in time to cross, and we were doomed to another lonely watch—yet the night passed quietly away without apprehension on our part or unusual incident.

In the morning we were joined by our friends and had a long drive, made doubly tedious by being compelled to go many miles out of our way to find a convenient crossing over one of the affluents of the Kansas. Evening found us weary, and with sharp appetites for a fine supper of prairie chickens, which are so abun-

dant that we are kept well supplied. The
monotony of the day was partially relieved
by the view of the prairie on fire, at a safe
distance on our right. The smoke rolled up
in angry-looking clouds, and I could distinguish fitful flashes and tongues of flame, as
it leaped along the ground. How terrible
to those surrounded by an ocean of such
flame, in the tall, dry grass, I could easily
appreciate.

During the day we passed a low, gravelly
bluff, from which issued a fine spring. A
generous volume of water gushed forth, which
made a beautiful little pebbly brook down
the bank and across the road. The well-
beaten path attested the number of visitors
to this fountain; and its cool waters contrasted
deliciously with the turbid pools from which
we have been compelled too often to quench
our thirst.

Yesterday we encountered another stream,
still more troublesome than that of the preceding day. It took the train two mortal
hours to get over, though it seemed to me
much longer, and involved the necessity of

unloading some of the wagons. During this, and while we were at dinner on the north bank of the stream, there was every appearance of a thunder storm. The clouds rolled up black and threatening, with peals of thunder; and the exhibition was doubly grand, from the vast expanse of view which we enjoyed. The storm, however, passed by, and the muttering thunder gradually died away in the distance.

Before we resumed our journey, a returning Californian, as he represented himself, rode into camp mounted on a serviceable-looking horse, and armed to the teeth. I was watching for an opportunity to send back a letter, but this man's appearance was so forbidding, that I would not trust him with it. He was surly and snappish, and seemed averse to giving a direct answer to any of the questions asked him. The captain inquired whether he had had any trouble from the Indians; he answered: " the white Indians are more troublesome than the red ones." After leaving us, there were various shrewd guesses in regard to him. One thought he had murdered and robbed his companion; another that he had

2*

never been to California, but was a mere marauder, ready to join the Indians in plundering any party of emigrants weak enough to be attacked with safety. Nothing too bad could be imagined of him, or else nature libeled him sadly in stamping his features.

The next day brought us to our present camping ground; and, as we are now wayfarers of ten days' standing, we have settled down into some kind of order in our nomadic life. The first thing, on stopping, is to unharness the mules, and place them where the feed is the most abundant; after which water and wood are procured, fires built, and our own meal prepared. While these things are in progress, I generally call on or receive a call from Mrs. Phelps; nor is the baby forgotten; and the little thing gets along wonderfully well, and is a general favorite.

The larder of a caravan like ours, where it is an object to have as little weight as may be, cannot be very extensive. Coffee, ham, and short-cake, and often cakes prepared from the pinola, form the staple of our meals— prairie chickens and ducks come in at frequent

intervals as luxuries. You would be astonished at the scanty supply of fuel with which
our meals are cooked, and the ease with which
it is accomplished. We have a stout board,
which, placed on the front seat of the carriage,
forms the table; the men stand up in front;
I keep my seat in the carriage, and make a
very convenient side table for myself with one
of the cushions. I am astonished at the keen
zest with which our humble fare is relished.
Coffee is an indispensable, is drunk in great
quantities, and seems to be a stimulus well
suited to this mode of life.

At night the guard is selected, the animals
picketed around the carriages, and the men,
with buffalo robes and blankets, bivouac upon
the ground. We house ourselves in the carriage; and, with its curtains closely strapped
down, have occasionally found it inconveni-
ently warm.

I have become better acquainted with our
traveling companions. We have a square,
stout, and rather bluff-looking, intelligent
young man by the name of Pierce, who is a
nephew of one of the nominees for the presi-

dency. He has been in a counting-room in Philadelphia, has traversed the Western States as a collecting agent, and is now, so far as I can learn, an amateur traveler. He has a ready, helping hand for the various emergencies of the train as they arise, and we thus far are much indebted to him for society and amusement.

Then we have a tall, lathy young lawyer by the name of Stringfellow, who claims to be in some way connected with good society somewhere in Virginia. By what singular freak of the floods of fortune he has been borne from the Old Dominion, and is now drifting with us towards Salt Lake, I do not know. He is very polite and obliging, and I am frequently amused by his rather pompous descriptions of upper-ten life in Virginia.

The rest of the men are hired hands belonging to the train; and, towards us, are kind and obliging. The only drawback is the terrible swearing in which they indulge, when provoked by the contumacy of the mules. The captain, who is a proficient in the same dialect, undertook one day to change the habits of

the men in this respect; but he swore so vigor-
ously himself, in telling them they should not
swear, that it only excited ridicule : and so I
fear we are to go on swearing all the way
through.

LETTER IV.

FORT KEARNEY, Saturday, Sept. 10, 1852.

My last letter brought down the narrative of our adventures to the 2d instant,
while we were encamped a short distance
from the Big Vermilion, which we crossed
the succeeding day. We found the banks
of that stream so very steep, that each wagon
and carriage had to be let down by ropes
fastened to the back wheels, and drawn
tightly around a tree by four or five men.
This formed a sufficient drawback, and yet
it seemed to me as if we must inevitably
pitch forward, pell-mell, over our team. We
passed over safely, however, and traveled to
and crossed the Big Blue, a clear, deep, and
rapid stream, encamping a little out of the

belt of tall trees, with which it is lined. I
could not avoid feeling timid when in the
middle, with the swift water surging up to
the carriage-body, the stumbling of the mules,
breaking of the harness, or other misadven-
ture, would have sadly disconcerted us—but
why doubt the guardianship of a kind Providence ?

We found here a grateful supply of good
water; but were most diligently attended with
a countless host of hungry musquitoes. A
musquito-bar, with which we are provided,
proved a sufficient protection, and secured us
a night of undisturbed repose. In the morning, we were startled with the news that four
mules were missing, two of which belonged
to our own carriage. The truants had wan-
dered off after daylight, and recrossed the
river, but were, after a short delay, recovered,
and we resumed our journey. This may seem
a trifling circumstance to you, but to us, surrounded by unseen, hostile savages, the idea
of losing the means of locomotion involved
consequences more serious than we were willing to contemplate.

There is a great deal of monotony in the journey, and yet something occurs each day which affords excitement. For the last few days we have seen more or less of the antelope, a wonderfully light, graceful animal. Sometimes there will be fifteen or twenty in a flock. On seeing us they will bound off a short distance, and then turn about and gaze at us for a few moments; and then they will fly like the wind until they disappear, over a swell in the prairie. Wolves, too, are becoming common, and will run a short space, on seeing us; but generally stop at a safe distance. At night, however, they give us an unfailing serenade—sometimes two or three, and at others a full band, keep up a wailing, plaintive sound, which is far from unpleasant.

We reached the Little Blue on the 7th, after seeing plenty of antelope, a plenty of wolves, and encountering a plenty of "*pitch-holes*." These pitch-holes are deep ravines, gullied out by the spring freshets, and are exceedingly deceptive and troublesome. The train will be traveling quietly along on level ground, when, suddenly, one vehicle after another will disappear, as though they had sunk into the ground; and when we come up we find one of these deep gullies, down which we too must plunge, to reappear on the opposite bank. Often the banks are steep and precipitous, and the wheels are to be locked, and we dismount to lighten the load or avoid the danger.

At one of our stopping places the stage from Salt Lake came up; and we were rejoiced to hand the driver a package of letters for home, with the comfortable assurance that they would reach their destination. Of course, he was plied with questions as to the Indians, the buffalo, the feed, etc. His report was favorable—his own safety being a confirmation in regard to the natives. The mail is under the charge of only two men, very daring and reckless in their appearance; but how they succeed in running the gauntlet of the Indians, is to me marvelous. Their movements are rapid, and they have plenty of spare mules at different stations on the route.

On the eighth we continued the route up

the Little Blue; and in the afternoon had a thunder-storm, which settled down into a steady rain. Much to my satisfaction, the carriage proved substantially water-tight, and we rode out the storm perfectly dry. The evening was drizzly and cheerless. As we approached our camping ground, we saw at the left, near the stream, a number of tents, with smoke curling lazily up among the trees, and mules scattered about feeding. Who were they, Pawnees or white men? They proved to be a party of men from Oregon, and had been sixty days on the route.

In the morning the Oregonians struck their tents and passed us while we were at breakfast. They were an odd looking company, dressed in all sorts of ways—one man had a gay serape, and a hat with the remains of a plume—it was crownless, however, and hair enough played about in the wind to furnish scalp-locks for a dozen war chiefs. They all had the dashing look of defiance so commonly found upon the plains, and I begin to think we look ditto. That the poor Indians are, year after year, receding before the tread of

the white man, is to me no longer a mystery.
A white frost might as well contend with the
advancing sun-beams, as the natives with the
race who are now rolling the tide of emigration into the Western World.

We resumed our journey, and leaving the
river, traveled over a rather bleak appearing,
undulating plain towards a ridge of low sand-
hills which forms the west bounds of the
valley of the Platte or Nebraska. You would
be perfectly astonished at the distance at which
objects are visible; and, owing to some pecu-
liarity of the atmosphere, they loom up, become distorted, and appear to be in motion.
Often half a dozen crows, ahead of us in the
road, will assume the appearance of a party
of men. We were one day excited in an un-
common degree by these illusions. A dark
object appeared on the rising ground at a
considerable distance in front. One said it
was a buffalo, another that it was a Pawnee;
and so much was I of the same opinion, that
I expected every moment to see him dart off
to apprise his companions of our approach.
The matter was debated pro and con with

no satisfactory solution; when lo! on coming up to this formidable, shapeless thing, it proved to be a battered piece of stove-pipe, lying by the side of a crownless hat, which had, in its dilapidated condition, been thrown away by some passing emigrant.

We reached and passed the sand bluffs, and encamped in the valley of the Platte. A long line of trees stretching east and west, a great many miles, indicated the river. Man and beast were made half crazy by that usua evening pest—the musquito. Cold weather will, at least, rid us of this troublesome annoyance. The howl of the wolf again lulled our senses into forgetfulness, and in the morning we went cheerily forward, with the expectation of making an early bivouac at Fort Kearney.

The fort was soon announced as being in sight. It assumed various fantastic shapes, and occasioned some speculation as to its identity. It looked like a rock, a mound of earth, a tower, a clump of branchless trees, or a huddle of buildings, at times, as fancy suggested. Pierce rode with us and amused

me with stories of their mode of living at
these forts—said there were no ladies, and
that they lived not much better than pigs.
We speculated whether the officers would
notice us enough to invite us to dinner; and
our lively companion concluded that, at all
events, these bachelor votaries of Mars would
leave me out of the list of their invitations.
We seemed forever approaching the establishment; a dead level plain, with no intervening
object, causing the distance to appear much
less than it really was. My lofty ideas of a
fort were doomed to be sadly disappointed.
I had a confused notion of massive granite
walls, and frowning battlements, surmounted
with cannon ready to belch forth their thunder; and surrounded with bastions and para-
pets, with grim visaged men, "bearded like
the pard," pacing to and fro with guns on
their shoulders. As we rode up I could not
help the conviction, that we had mistaken
a trading-post for this fortress—but it was
Fort Kearney and nothing else.

The principal building was a two-storied
dwelling with a stoop in front—in fact, it

appeared on the outside like a neat and comfortable farm-house. In the vicinity was a low, mud building, which might easily be mistaken for an ice-house, but was, in reality, the magazine. Then there were low ranges of buildings for barracks, store-house, stables, etc. As we approached near, some persons were standing on the upper stoop: they soon left, however; and, when we halted, a very gentlemanly looking man, in citizen dress, came up to the carriage, and introduced himself as Captain Wharton. This was accompanied by an invitation to come directly in to dinner, in a way which precluded all possibility of a refusal. I was wholly taken aback. At the entrance we were met by Mrs. Wharton, who gave me a very cordial embrace, and we were ushered into a prettily furnished parlor. I was completely bewildered, and hardly knew what I said or did. I had never dreamed there was anything civilized about a fort—I had only thought of officers living in a very rude, boisterous sort of way—but here, we were in the very midst of refinement. We were soon seated at table; and, in its substantial and luxurious appliances, found an agreeable contrast, to our rambling camp accommodations.

Mrs. W. is lady-like, intelligent, and very sociable. We have talked, incessantly, about everybody and everything, past, present, and to come. There is a kindliness about both of them which gushes out to overflowing; and they absolutely seem grateful to us for coming, as objects to be warmed by the sunshine of their dispositions. Everything is neat and orderly about them. There is a large, well-cultivated vegetable and flower garden; and, adjacent to it, an immense field of corn—and everything wears the appearance of the establishment of a wealthy farmer. All the skeldering and swaggering indications which, somehow, entered into my preconceived ideas of a common soldier, are entirely wanting among the rank and file. I have, to be sure, seen but few of them, but they were quietly attending to some duty, about in the same way that you would expect to see an orderly set of people engaged in out-door avocations. Yet we are, occasionally, reminded of the character of our host, by the short, ringing tones of military discipline. We were indulging in a lively chat after tea, when we heard a firm, measured tread in the hall, and a man with a musket and bayonet, presented himself at the door, brought his gun to a salute, made his report, and received his commands for the evening. This accomplished officer, evidently, has a moral as well as military control over his men. He related to us many interesting anecdotes of his dealings with the Pawnees. When an outrage occurs, he promptly sends some men to their head-quarters, and brings in their chief a prisoner, in which condition the savage is compelled to remain, until the matter is satisfactorily explained or redressed.

There was a Pawnee lad domesticated in the family—the first of the tribe we have seen. His organ of destructiveness is, according to phrenology, immensely large. I asked him if he would kill me, provided he had a good opportunity, and could gain anything by it; and the scamp unhesitatingly answered yes, with a grin.

We proposed to sleep, as usual, in our car-

riage, but Mrs. W. assumed military preroga-
tives, and would not listen to it; so we had
only to yield ourselves prisoners of war, "rescue or no rescue."

I am now finishing my letter, while preparations for departure are going on around me.
Our more than kind friends have made themselves familiar with our wants, and are laying
us under obligations, impressing upon us sundry necessaries and luxuries for the journey.
To show how thoughtful they are as to our
comforts, I will mention the case of our lantern. Among the traps brought from St.
Louis, was an old-fashioned, lumbering tin
lantern. As an incident of the journey, this
beautiful piece of furniture got crushed out
of all shape, into that of a cocked-hat, which
is the universal soubriquet for all shapeless
things. Of course this was a great loss; but
here we are supplied with a much more convenient article.

We have to start now in a few minutes,
and Captain W. has his carriage at the door,
intending to accompany us some ten miles
on the road. I had like to have forgotten,

most unwomanly, I confess, to mention two
beautiful, bright boys, belonging to this model
garrison.   One of them is now at my elbow,
and is destined to be a warrior; for yesterday
he was mounted on a Cheyenne pony, with
bow and arrows, which he teased me to see
him shoot.

But I hear Morse shouting, "all ready,"
and must bring this to a close.

LETTER V.

WARD & GARAY'S STATION, }
Seven miles west of Fort Laramie, }
Monday, 27th Sept., 1852.

WE are now recruiting for a day at a trading station a short distance west of Fort Laramie, and about six hundred and fifty miles from Independence. Our camp is about a mile from the establishment; and, while the men are mending harness, shoeing mules, and overhauling all things and sundry for a fresh start, I will, for your benefit, connect together some of the links of our chain of travel to this point.

The journey hither has been of extreme interest. We have abounded in buffalo, antelope, wolves, prairie dogs, Indians, and, above all, the most magnificent scenery; and I am heartily tired of all except the last.

We parted from our kind friends at Fort Kearney on the 10th, and pursued the route along the south bank of the Platte. As we were entering the buffalo country, every one was on the alert to catch a view of that celebrated animal; every distant bush, rock, tree, or other dark object was gazed at, and the question mooted as to whether it was, or was not, until finally the huge animal, in very deed, burst upon our vision. Since then we have seen thousands upon thousands. They first appeared in small, scattered squads, and gave the impression of cattle quietly grazing in their pastures; but, as we neared them, they ran away with a stiff, awkward gait, until they disappeared over the sand bluffs. We had a terrible fright the very day of leaving the fort. Our carriage happening to be in the advance, we came suddenly so near three or four huge creatures that had been concealed from our view in a hollow, that Denton undertook to shoot one. He walked boldly up towards the animal and fired, with no apparent effect; the buffalo raised his head and stood gazing at us. As Denton was walking leisurely back, the buffalo scampered off, and pretty soon he cast away the gun, and ran towards us in the wildest alarm, crying out—" the wolves! the wolves!" It was high time; those behind us had commenced a *stampede;* ours caught the alarm and started; but he succeeded in catching hold of the leaders, and Mr. F. held firmly to the reins—I assisted at the expense of a pair of blistered hands. The team was checked in a few rods, but those in the rear whirled past like the wind. We just escaped utter demolition as it seemed to me, by one of the heavy wagons which grazed us in passing. Fortunately, the mules were too heavily burdened to escape, and were stopped after running about half a mile. No damage resulted, except a slight injury to one of the wagons. This was my first practical knowledge of a stampede, though not the last.

The next day we encamped on Plum Creek; and a Mexican, whose services were engaged by Capt. Phelps at the fort, killed a fine cow,

and our fare was mended by the far-famed
buffalo meat; this with some mushrooms
freshly gathered, made a feast fit for an
epicure. This Mexican, who answers to the
name of *Jo*, our camp English for José (Hosa),
proves to be a capital hunter.

The river is full of small islands of drifting
sand, and is as much discolored as the Missouri.
Necessity, however, knows no law; and we
have been compelled to use it for drinking
and cooking for hundreds of miles. Grand
Island, however, is an exception to the general
rule, commencing at Kearney and extending
about sixty miles.

While at Plum Creek, a corps of 160
mounted riflemen, with a train of baggage-
wagons, passed us going towards the fort,
and made a very imposing appearance. The
captain rode up to our carriage, and very
civilly inquired whether we had any sickness
in our company. They pitched their tents
about a mile from us; their camp-fires soon
flickered in the thickening darkness; and the
sound of the French horn, mellowed by the
distance, floated over us, mingling its rich

music with the howling of the wolf. Two
wagons of returning emigrants were traveling
under the protection of this force; with them
was a woman, who had started in the spring,
with her husband and six children for Oregon.
She had buried one child, ten years old, on
the Platte, and her husband a little beyond
Salt Lake; and, completely discouraged, she
had thus far made her way back with the
surviving children, dependent upon the charity
of emigrants. She told her story in a simple,
artless manner, which vouched for its truth,
and strongly excited my sympathy in her favor.
She tried to tell me where her child's grave
might be found, that we could, at least, let
fall upon it a tear of regret in passing. Alas!
it will be difficult to distinguish the resting
place of this poor child, in the multitude of
graves which line the road. The further we
go, the more frequent they become; and we
are fast growing callous to the mortality and
suffering, of which they furnish such abundant
evidence. What a history they unfold! Some
are found close by the way-side, as if its poor
tenant had been hurriedly and carelessly in-

humed by strangers; others appear a little further off upon a slight mound, or under a solitary tree, as though its occupant had been laid in its lonely resting place by surviving friends amid tears and anguish—its future guardian, the roving red man—its future requiem, the howling of the wolf.

The next evening we had a storm of rain, with a gale strong enough to blow us into the river. We made things very snug, however; and, bidding defiance to the fury of the elements, very composedly read ourselves to sleep by the light of the new lantern.

I will not tire your patience by a description of each day's adventures—a general outline will be sufficient. We pursued our way up the Platte, finding the buffalo more and more abundant, until we crossed the South Fork of the river;—in some instances there would be thousands in a drove. Sometimes they would be scattered far and near on the bluffs on both sides of the river, and seemed like the cattle upon the thousand hills. They invariably ran off as we approached—the calves scampering faster than the elders. One day

I was terribly frightened. We were passing along near the bluffs, and, by a turn of the road, came suddenly upon an immense herd of these monsters of the plains, between us and the river. They started and run in three mighty streams, two of which went directly through the gaps in our train. As they thundered past in blind fear, shaking the very ground beneath their feet, it seemed to me as though everything must be dashed in pieces. I thought I could then realize something of the terrific appearance of a charge of cavalry. Two of the teams dashed out after them, but were soon checked without injury.

We crossed the South Fork on the 20th, and since then we have not seen a single buffalo; though antelope and wolves continue plenty as ever. This crossing was a subject of dread for some days: we were told of dangerous quick sands, which sometimes utterly swamped the traveler; the water, however, was low, and we had no trouble.

The country between this ford and the North Fork is an uneven barren. We traversed it, however, in one day; and, for the last

3*

five miles, found it broken up into precipitous ridges and hillocks, composed of spongy lime-stone. We finally descended into Ash Hollow —a beautiful and romantic ravine, with cedar, ash, and clematis—which led us to the river on which we encamped. From this point all the way up the stream, the interest in the scenery has not flagged for a single moment.

The first striking feature was the celebrated Court House Rock, as it is called—an immense pile of reddish sand stone, which, standing alone upon the plain, appears like a gigantic ruin. It is quite impossible to divest yourself of the idea, in passing, that this was erected by human hands. You could distinguish, in front, a huge rotunda; windows upon the sides; the remains of different roofs, and a cupola—but, as we were never nearer than seven miles (as the captain said), there was plenty of room for the imagination. Soon after, the equally celebrated Chimney Rock made its appearance like an obelisk, towering its solitary shafts to the sky. We were tired of gazing upon this wonderful curiosity; but I will not waste words in attempting to present you a picture of what has been so well described by Fremont and others. In passing, it looked so near, that I, with Mr. F., started to walk to it, thinking we could easily do so, and overtake the train. After walking half a mile we seemed to have made no progress towards the object of our curiosity, and gave it up—much to the amusement of Morse, who halted the carriage for us, while the others had gone on a mile in advance.

The Court House and Chimney Rocks are not alone—they are only remarkable objects in a scenery of wonderful magnificence, scattered over a distance of about one hundred miles. We left the river before reaching Scott's Bluff, and passed through a narrow valley, lined with rocky bluffs of a similar character, washed and worn into a vast variety of forms, which fancy aided in fashioning into ruined works of art—turrets—towers—castles, etc. On the right was one which attracted my attention quite as much as any of the rest—it was a huge, cylindrical shaped rock as a base, surmounted by two others.

Emerging from this collection of curiosities, we again came to the river, and soon found ourselves involved in a perfect rabble of Indians. We passed two villages of Cheyenne lodges, and the whole population poured out, and not only surrounded, but followed us for more than a mile; and they were of all sorts and sizes, from infancy to old age. One large Indian I fancied to be a chief. He kept close to the carriages, as being the post of honor, which none presumed to interfere with, and strode along with great majesty. He had a bunch of gay feathers on his head; leggins with wide fringe; and a beautiful skin, painted and worked with beads, gathered gracefully around his shoulders, the ends of which trailed in the dirt, with as much fashion as the skirts of a city belle. Occasionally I could see him glancing at his adornments, to be sure that the trailing was a-la-mode Cheyenne.

The men were, many of them, armed; and, as the captain motioned them off, some of them made a threatening exhibition of the iron heads upon their arrows. The children were as frolicksome and tatterdemalion as those more civilized. Some of the girls were pretty, in spite of vermilion and other etcetera. Judging from the dress of these natives, there must be quite as much distinction of caste among them as with our squires, colonels, and honorables—the canaille here being very much unencumbered with dress of any kind. A band of nearly naked youngsters were mounted on ponies, and riding to and fro with the utmost apparent recklessness.

We encamped near enough to Fort Laramie to hear the roll of the evening drum. Some nursery rhymer has said, in language most eloquent to us, when children:

> " I hate that drum's discordant sound,
>   Parading around, and round, and round."

But, however much its rumbling tones may usually be associated with scenes of violence and blood, it, for once, furnished sweet music to the ear—it indicated the presence of our countrymen under the stars and stripes, and protection against the savages, whose whooping annoyed us the whole evening.

The next morning we came up to the fort,

which proved to be a more extensive establishment than Kearney. The commandant was
out hunting; and, while Capt. Phelps and Mr.
F. were engaged at the commissary department in replenishing our wasting stores, one
of the subordinate officers came up to the
carriage, and made himself politely sociable.
You see I am becoming familiar with military
terms—in fact, I feel myself at times quite
Amazonian.

Our stay was short, and we hurried on to
the present station, where it seems some mules
are to be purchased to replace those which
have been worn down by hard service and
scanty feed. We get very discouraging news
in regard to the grass, for the rest of the
journey: all agree that it has been used up
by the immense summer emigration, and the
time is too much advanced to permit us to
diverge from the usual route. The captain
says he will get through, but Mundy wears a
long face; and I can easily see that it is a
subject of anxious discussion.

We are now encamped directly on the bank
of the river, under two fine trees. The station,

about a mile below, is in a handsome bend of the stream, and consists of two or three log buildings, with a large one of stone, about half erected. All the men have gone there except "Doc," of whom I have before made mention, leaving Mrs. Phelps, the baby, and myself nearly alone. Some half a dozen Indians, and as many squaws, have been hanging around all day. One, a tall, stout-looking Cheyenne, has a buffalo robe around him, very handsomely worked with quills and beads, native fashion. I have been trying the last hour to trade with him. They all understand the word *swap;* so I held up my red shawl, pointed to his robe, and said, "*swap.*" He commenced pulling it from his shoulders, then shook his head. I put on the shawl, and made various manœuvres to show what a superior thing it was, but it would not do. I then added a blanket to the shawl; he examined it for some time, and I began to think the trade would be effected, when he again shook his head. He then discovered a demijohn in the carriage, and cried out, "*whisk, whisk,*" and began again to pull off the robe. I then

motioned them off, but found them disposed
to be troublesome, and had finally to call in
aid to get rid of them. They have just
gone off muttering, and I am finishing my
letter ready for a start. These poor creatures
will part with anything for liquor.

Before closing, I will mention that we have
heard some not very encouraging stories about
the Mormons. It is said they do really practice polygamy; and some of the traders we
meet express regret that Mr. F. has brought
his wife along, fearing it may lay the foun-
dation for the same difficulties that occurred
with the former officers. The story is, that
the wife of the former secretary was invited
to a house where there were six women with
young babies, all belonging to one husband,
and that she took offense at it. I find, however, there is a difference of opinion among
the gentry—some of whom acquit the lady of
all agency in the matter, and contend that
Brigham Young had made up his mind to
get rid of them on any pretext. I sometimes
fear we shall find ourselves in a nest of hor-
nets; but I mean to be very obtuse—regarding

myself simply as a traveler among a strange people, and treat all alike—the same as though we were going to Japan or China.

It is said, also, that letters are tampered with at their post-office; and this reminds me to request you to say nothing offensive to them in your letters to us; and mind and seal them with sealing wax. Captain Phelps says there is no danger, and insures us kind treatment. I do not mean to give myself any uneasiness. I have already heard of so many bugbears, which, when faced, proved to be neither bugs nor bears, that I am becoming very much hardened to all apprehensions of danger.

LETTER VI.

LARAMIE PEAK—SNOW STORM—INDIAN VIL-
LAGE—TRAIN OF MORMON MISSIONARIES—
WILD SAGE—ALKALINE EFFLORESCENCES—
INDEPENDENCE ROCK—DEVIL'S GATE—RAT-
TLESNAKE MOUNTAINS—GLOOMY PROSPECTS
—SOUTH PASS, AND WIND RIVER MOUNTAINS
—PACIFIC SPRINGS—GREEN RIVER.

TRADING PORT, on Green River, Oct. 16, 1852.

WE left Ward and Garay's station, near
Fort Laramie, on the 28th of September, a
mild, pleasant day. For a number of days,
Laramie peak had been in view a little to the
southwest—a landmark of great interest; the
snowy summit of which was occasionally lit
up by the morning sun with roseate hues.
The country entirely lost its character of
plains, and was decidedly hilly; we were fairly
in the suburbs, so to speak, of the great Rocky
Mountain range.

We continued up the Platte, crossing it
three times before we finally left that river.

the country becoming more and more rough. On the north side we found numerous instances of a bright red rock cropping out on the sides of the hills, sometimes in regular strata, and at others in a confused manner, with scattered cedar and fir, presenting a very beautiful appearance. The weather became exceedingly changeable. On the evening of the first of October we had a violent cold rain, changing to snow before morning, which broke gloomily enough, with four inches of heavy, damp snow on the ground. The mules had a wretched night of it, and we began to realize what might be our condition in this elevated region, with deep snow and failing animals. The clouds cleared away about nine o'clock, and the snow gradually disappeared, except upon the hill tops; but the roads were heavy, and before night, three mules utterly gave out. Poor things! their food had become scanty, and yet we could not stop a moment—our lives depended on going forward.

Every day we have had more or less of the natives around us, generally mounted on

ponies, and sometimes exceedingly troublesome, While at dinner on Deer Creek, some
ten or a dozen annoyed us: one had on a
pair of green goggles, which he wore just
above his eyes. We enjoyed a hearty laugh at
his expense, yet he evidently prided himself on
this badge of distinction, quite as much as a
Russian Count glittering with the stars of his
order; and, surely, the Indian has quite as good
right to his gew-gaw as the European.

On the same day we passed a collection of
lodges, on an island in the river, under a grove
of fine trees—the view was extremely picturesque. They were the best looking we had
seen; and the chief's lodge could easily be
distinguished. They were engaged in drying
buffalo meat, large quantities of which were
strung upon poles. On spying our cavalcade,
large numbers ran to the river and dashed
in; but, owing to the deepness of the water,
only a few crossed over. These, with the
party already with us, scampered around on
their ponies, in a sort of helter-skelter fashion,
nodding and grinning, and trying to shake
hands with the men. At a little distance off,

dressed in gay blankets, and mounted on their ponies, they look fanciful enough; but the romance of Indian life will not bear a closer inspection—they are neither more nor less than filthy savages.

The Black Mountain range was on our left, covered with snow. On the fourth we halted on the south bank of the river, at the last crossing-place, amid the scattered fragments of wagons, remnants of camp fires, decaying bones of animals, and other indicia of the spot, as a species of eddy in the great current of emigration, coursing from the east to the west. While "*nooning*" at this point, a large train of covered wagons hove in sight, and wound slowly over the bluffs on the other side, making a very singular appearance. We counted thirty, as one after the other came into view. They soon passed over, and proved to be a train of Mormon missionaries, eighteen days from Salt Lake. They had fine teams; the men appeared friendly, and manifested a good deal of pleasure in meeting us, saying, among other things, that Mr. F. had been looked for at their city for some time. I had lately heard so many vile things of these Mormons, that I expected to see some of them, at least, adorned with cloven feet. I begin to think they are no worse or better than other communities. They addressed each other as brothers, which sounded pleasant. Orson Pratt, said to be a very noted champion among them, was in the company.

After leaving the Platte, the country became still more rough and diversified, and the traveling more laborious. We passed over a barren region of sand and wild sage, the grass becoming continually more scanty, and our poor mules gradually wearing down. The weather, however, grew quite warm again for two or three days. On the fifth, at evening, we had thunder-storms all around, with only a slight sprinkling at our camp; but the morning of the sixth was ushered in by a cold, raw, northwest wind; and, during the day, it blew a fierce gale, annoying us prodigiously with the drifting sand. At noon we stopped in a collection of sage bushes, sufficiently large to partially protect us from the wind, but I found the buffalo steak too much seasoned with sand to be agreeable, notwithstanding the assurance of Morse, that such seasoning was not only clean but healthy.

Among the peculiarities of the region which attracted our attention, were white alkaline efflorescences, in different places, as though flour had been scattered upon the ground. Occasionally the incrustations were of sufficient thickness to gather it up in pieces, and it is collected for use as saleratus; and pools of water in the vicinity appeared of the color of common lye. We passed two ponds strongly impregnated with alkali, in one of which two famished mules, belonging to one of the heavy wagons, fell flat, and were with difficulty rescued from drowning—the poor things looked sorry enough after their disagreeable bath; and if swearing could have done any good, would have been speedily restored to flesh and activity.

On the evening of the sixth we encamped under Independence Rock, on the Sweet Water, and had the protection of its huge buttresses against the cold wind. It was a wet, dismal, cheerless evening; wood was too scanty to make more than one fire, and that a poor affair. We crept into our dormitory at an early hour, and were agreeably disappointed in the morning, in not finding the ground covered with snow. This rock is an immense pile, over a mile in circuit as they said; but I cannot believe that. It is cracked, seamed, and fissured in every possible way, and, in fact, may be described as a collection of enormous granite boulders. But oh! the names written upon its massy sides. If everybody does not secure immortality, there is no enduring virtue in tar, or granite. We amused ourselves with the frequent recurrence of particular cognomens, such as Smith, and Johnson. There was no lack of oddities either, such as Scroggins, Tenpenny, and Vanderwittle. Doubtless, vanity has had much to do with these clumsy inscriptions; but they seem, after all, to have served the use of a kind of traveling directory, inasmuch as Mr. Smith, in passing, can ascertain, if he have the patience, when particular members of his numerous brotherhood have traveled the same road.

Shortly after leaving Independence Rock,

we passed within a short distance of the Devil's Gate—a deep, narrow cut, directly through the rocks, and through which the Sweet Water surges with great violence. It was my settled intention to have visited this great curiosity, but half of the train were sick with chills and fever, and, among the rest, Mr. F., a circumstance which I have before omitted to mention, to save you from anxiety; and the Captain felt that he could not spare a moment for sight-seeing. This deep cut cuts off the south end of a high rocky range, called the Rattlesnake Mountains; and as we passed around it, and while, too, the train stopped for fifteen minutes at a trading-station to purchase some brown sugar, which proved to be half Indian meal, I managed to obtain a good distant view of the water gushing forth from its pent-up channel. You must not imagine a great river like the Hudson or Susquehanna—every stream here is a river, and the Sweet Water is scarcely as large as the inlet of our own Cayuga Lake.

For three days we had the Rattlesnake Hills

4

on our right—a huge range of granite—on the
left, in the distance, were the peaks of the
Black Hills, and the snowy tops of the Wind
River Mountains began to show themselves
at the northwest. It is difficult to describe
the scenery; there was no one thing that
engrossed attention—but nature put on a
massive grandeur in all directions. There was
nothing little—it was all great—the Olympian
Jove might well have held there his court,
with Titans for his subjects. The sensations
were peculiar; you feel lifted up out of yourself; everything seems enduring; and you
think that earthquakes and volcanoes might
there spend their fury in vain. The hills
around our delightful village became dwarfed
down into mere bluffs—very pretty, to be
sure, with their cultivated farms and patches
of woodland, but very, very diminutive.

On the ninth we met the stage, in company
with a gentleman, in another carriage, by the
name of Kinkead, of the firm of Livingston
& Kinkead. Of course, all parties came to
a halt, to shake hands and talk over the
news—the grass was reported to be scanty,

and the party had encountered snow in the South Pass—cold news for us.

The weather continued to be variable, and we were still east of the South Pass: a heavy snow there would effect a disastrous blockade of our movements. I never shall forget the evening of the 10th—the clouds had thickened all the afternoon, and brought on a cold, northeast rain. The mules had a dismal prospect for supper, and before we retired the rain had become sleet. I slept but little that night, and, as the sharp sound of sleet on the carriage-top died away, I fancied the snow thickly falling. There we were, nearly a thousand miles from Missouri, with the dreaded Pass before us; perhaps a foot of snow to struggle through in the morning, with unrefreshed animals, and to crown all, my husband sick. I felt so wretchedly gloomy, that it was exceedingly difficult to revive a calm reliance upon the divine Providence.

In the morning, however, we found a thick fog and only an inch of melting snow upon the ground; and Denton, who was on the night-watch, cheered us by stating that the mules had found some good feed on a hill-side near the camp. We rose up with thankful hearts. The morning would have been dismal and cheerless, under other circumstances; but a great burden had been taken from our apprehensions of danger, and the whole train manifested as much cheerful gayety as though the " sun, new risen," were spreading his genial glories around us.

We started full of hope—about ten the mist cleared off, and we had a fine day. We pushed rapidly forward, and that evening encamped at the base of some rugged highlands, which form, as it were, the last step before reaching the summit. The clouds gathered at evening, portending a storm. In this, however, we were again agreeably disappointed, and the next day, facing a cutting northwester, we found ourselves within that celebrated gateway of the mountains—the South Pass.

The snow which had fallen some days before had disappeared, except in scattered patches. As we rounded the highlands, the Wind River Mountains rose up into full view. And these were a portion of the far-famed Rocky Mountains, upon whose snowy tops I have little dreamed it would be my fortune to gaze. There is a wonderful grandeur about them. There they repose in cold, glittering majesty, throwing back the rays of the sun upon the vision of the beholder, as if defiant of warmth. These were, indeed, mountains, lifting their hoary heads above the clouds, which were whirled along its sides in angry masses by the fierce winds. They have a wintry clothing of scattered evergreens about two-thirds the way up; the rest is snow, and this gave them very much the appearance of thunder clouds. You feel awed by their steady, immovable presence, and wait, in silence, for them to utter their deep voices.

This huge range of piled-up grandeur was a constant object of observation, which, for the time, swallowed up all else. The mind seemed to be constantly on the strain to compass the idea of its greatness. All other things —the scanty feed—the worn-down mules—the dangers which surrounded us, were of the earth, earthy. Before us, high and lifted up, was an enduring memorial power—it was a remove from the grossness of earth—an approach to the purity of heaven. At evening, as the sun receded to its resting-place, the spectacle of beauty in sublimity was past all power of description. As the earth darkened around us, the lofty peaks were lightened up by a refulgent glory, which flickered and finally disappeared, like the last flashes of an expiring volcano. As in the evening they were the last to bid farewell to the setting, so in the morning they were the first to greet the rising sun; and, as the gushing rays flashed around them, the whole firmament was filled with golden light.

On the 13th we crossed the Sweet Water, at that point a mere brook, for the last time. The road, from being exceedingly rough, with jagged rocks cropping out, and shooting up on all sides, became level and smooth as a village avenue; and, after rolling along pleasantly for some ten miles, Capt. Phelps apprised us that we were beginning to descend towards the Pacific. We had passed the summit of a continent. The air was remarkably pure and bracing, and contributed to a buoyancy of feeling which was, of course, aided with the idea that we were comparatively safe. We had been rarely favored—a week earlier would have exposed us to the snow-storm spoken of by Mr. Kinkead. It soon became manifest that the country beyond was below us, and I fancied the air to be milder.

We came that evening to the Pacific Springs, and encamped on a beautiful little trout stream, one of the sources of the Colorado, and very rapid, as though it knew how far it had to travel.

I had somehow got the idea, that once on the western slope of the Rocky Mountains, and everything would be found as smooth as a house floor; but we were as much involved in a system of rivers, highlands, and mountains as ever. We passed any number of streams—Big Sandy, Little Sandy, Ham's Fork, Black's Fork; indeed, there is now a perfect confusion in my recollection on the subject, and, not having a map before me, I shall not try to clear it up. One stream, I recollect, had cut a fearful chasm, almost as deep as Niagara, below the falls. We descended by a winding road, passed some distance along its bed, and, by dint of some extra hard pulling by the mules, reached the opposite bank. It was a wild scene.

As we progressed from day to day, the mountains receded to the right and back, and at evening flashed back the most beautiful rainbow tints. One evening we had a fine moonlight view; there it lay, white, cold, and stern, an image of grandeur without beauty. In a moralizing mood, you might well fancy it a tribunal of justice with no touch of mercy.

We forded Green River yesterday, a clear, rapid, and beautiful stream, belted with a fine growth of timber, and, at an early hour, encamped near a Canadian French trading-post, in a large bend of the river. In a short time Major Holman, the Indian agent, came up, and made our acquaintance, and invited Mr. F. to go with him on a short fishing excursion. It happened to be his well day, and the result of the expedition was a very welcome lot of trout for supper and breakfast. To-day Capt. Phelps is selling a portion of the goods in his charge to the traders, and Mr. F. is trying to get rid of our baggage-wagon, which, for the last two hundred miles, has been threatening a total shipwreck, without benefit of insurance. These business matters require time for negotiation and consummation, and will, probably, detain us the entire day. I take advantage of this delay to finish my letter.

I have taken pains to learn something of the men engaged in this out-of-the-way trading-post. They are living with Indian wives, who wait upon them—I saw one go to the river for water with a babe on her back. Around them are a gang of Indians and nonde-scripts, who ride about, hurry-skurry, in the most desperate fashion. During the whole of last night, as it seemed to me, they were whooping, shouting, and swearing; and, alto-gether, come as near to my conceptions of what the population of the infernal shades may well be as anything we have yet seen. I shall really be rejoiced if we escape un-harmed from their neighborhood. Yet the station is of signal benefit to us—we get some capital fresh beef, and renew our stock of flour,

4*

The Captain says they have large sums of money ; that he saw thousands of dollars lying on their table, last evening, while the principals were gambling. It is their passion to gather large herds of cattle, and the broad valley of the river furnishes unlimited grazing.

LETTER VII.

GREAT SALT LAKE CITY, Oct. 30, 1852.

THE date of my letter will assure you of
our safe arrival; and, now that we are here,
I can hardly recall the serious anticipations
of disaster which we have suffered.

After leaving the Valley of Green River, we
gained a more distinct view of the mountains
which bound the Great Basin on the east, and
to surmount which became, for more than a
week, the especial dread of the train. There
was the Big Mountain, and the Little Mountain, and all sorts of mountains which we were
bound to cross; and perhaps they would be
covered with snow.

On the evening of the 19th we encamped

at Fort Bridger—a long, low, strongly-con-
structed log building, surrounded by a high wall
of logs, stuck endwise in the ground. Bridger
came out and invited us in, and introduced
us to his Indian wife, and showed us his half-
breed children—keen, bright-eyed little things
Everything was rude and primitive. This
man strongly attracted my attention; there
was more than civility about him—there was
native politeness. He is the oldest trapper in
the Rocky Mountains; his language is very
graphic and descriptive, and he is evidently a
man of great shrewdness. He alarmed us in
regard to our prospects of getting through;
said the season had arrived when a heavy snow
might be looked for any day; urged us to
stay with him all winter; showed us where
we could lodge, guarded against the cold with
plenty of buffalo skins; and assured us that
he could make the benefit of our society and
the assistance of Mr. F., in his business, more
than compensate for the expenses of living.
This was a delicate way of offering the hospi-
talities of his establishment without remunera-
tion,

His wife was simplicity itself. She exhibited some curious pieces of Indian embroidery, the work of her own hands, with as much pleased hilarity as a child; and gave me a quantity of raisins and sauce berries—altogether, it was a very pleasant interview. He told us, if we were determined to go, to make as little delay as possible; and made a very acceptable addition to our larder, in the shape of fresh potatoes and other vegetables.

We left Bridger's early in the morning of the 20th, and, after traveling about ten miles, passed down a hill—very long, very steep, very rocky, and very bad—into a delightful valley some two miles wide, with two streams, which, I think, they called Muddy Forks—confluents of Bear River, and, of course, waters which belong to the Great Basin. While at dinner in this valley, a long train of wagons, drawn by oxen, came winding down the hill, and passed us—they were Mormons, with machinery for the manufacture of beet sugar. We soon passed them in turn, and took up our lodgings for the night on very high ground, among high sage bushes, with which we soon had bright fires, shooting forth long flames in the fresh breeze.

The next day we forded Bear River with some difficulty—the stream was rapid, and the bed full of large round stones, which made it troublesome for the mules to maintain their footing. After leaving the river, we entered upon a remarkable series of gorges and cañons, presenting a great variety of beautiful scenery, of which a prominent feature was the different colored rocks, washed into enormous columns, pedestals, porticoes, turrets, etc. It would be altogether too tedious to describe a tithe of it, though very attractive to us in passing. Echo Cañon was the most remarkable in all respects. It was said, by Capt. Phelps, to be thirty miles long, and certainly could not have averaged over half a mile in width; and was completely walled in, both sides—on the right by perpendicular rocks, washed into all sorts of shapes; and on the left by steep, irregular, rounded bluffs. Through the whole length flowed a small stream—a tributary of the Weber; and it seemed to me that we must have crossed it at least twenty times—and

some of the crossings were dreadfully troublesome. Near the lower end it narrowed into
a mere rocky gorge, and we were compelled
to pass over the bluffs at the left. Occasionally there would be a lateral cañon, with a
small brook. Into one of these we turned
and spent a night, in which there was a combination of wildness in "the heavens above,
and in the earth beneath." Wolves appeared
on the craggy peaks, almost over our heads,
and made a dismal complaint of hunger; a
thunder storm arose, the clouds rolling up in
angry masses; and, amid flashes of lightning,
peals of thunder, and pattering rain, we passed
quietly into the land of dreams—"the world
forgetting," if not "by the world forgot."

The next day we crossed the Weber, and
passed into East Cañon, which proved to be
full of disagreeables throughout. The road
was up and down continually; a rain storm
came up in the afternoon, which continued
during a portion of the night; at evening we
got involved in a thick grove of aspen, and
were compelled to encamp among the dripping
trees, from the impossibility of making our

way out in the darkness—a place peculiarly dangerous had any hostile Indians been prowling around; but we had overtaken a small party of Mormons going to Salt Lake, and felt comparatively safe. Everything was so wet that we had great difficulty in starting fires, and it was, altogether, cheerless enough.

The next day the road grew worse—it was bad every way—it was sidling, muddy, rocky, and full of sharp pitches—and then, too, we had to cross, I don't know how many times, a brawling stream, which seemed to be out of temper with us and everything else.

We finally came to a point where the road turned sharp to the right, and we stopped for dinner and rest, preparatory to climbing the "Big Mountain." Well, on we went—up, up, up, a steady, unbroken ascent of four miles. Oh! how weary were our poor worn-down mules in that fearful up-hill struggle: in the last mile, which was much the steepest, we had to give them frequent breathing-spells. I wished myself a little more ethereal than the facts would warrant, for the benefit of the tired brutes.

We reached the summit at sunset. It had commenced snowing; for a moment we caught a glimpse into the valley of the Great Salt Lake, but the storm and darkness increasing, shut everything from view. The two carriages were considerably in advance of the heavy wagons, and it became a matter of anxious consultation whether we should encamp on this cold, narrow, windy peak for the night, or plunge down the steep road in search of a more convenient bivouac. The woods here were somewhat dense, increasing the darkness; and, for the first time, Morse manifested some fear at the idea of driving down the cavernous-looking way before us. We soon proved our Yankee origin by "going ahead."

The wheels of the carriages were locked, and away we went. We halted in the first break in the extreme steepness, and held a council of war. Capt. Phelps, for some days, had been suffering from chills and fever, and was so unwell that he was afraid he could not keep the road. It was finally settled that Mr. F. should go forward as a guide, and Mrs. P. and I joined him, because we were afraid to ride. So on we went, stumbling over stones and rough places, and splashing through water-courses—and all the time fearful that the mules and carriages would come plunging pell-mell upon us. The imagination added to my share of the trouble. This mountain was said to be a favorite resort for grisly bears; and who could tell but we might all be crunched down by one of these monsters, without a moment's warning?

I began to think if we had not seen "the elephant," we were in a fair way of coming in contact with a very respectable substitute. Matters looked decidedly tragic, but ended in a more comic fashion; for, after stumbling along for about a mile, we came to a place less steep, got quietly into the carriages, rode on to a comfortable camping place, and laughed over the adventure, of which the most serious upshot was, our splashed and soiled garments. I became quite convinced that the fashions of the Bloomer sisterhood were decidedly to be preferred in similar emergencies.

The contents of a revolver were fired into

the air, to apprise the rest of the party of our whereabouts; and, comically enough, two or three of the men came running down, thinking we were actually engaged

> " ——————— with beasts of prey,
> Or men more wild and fierce than they."

Fortunately we were here met by a team from the merchants in the valley to whom the goods of the train belonged, with oats for our famished mules, and fresh butter and eggs for ourselves. We soon had a rousing fire by a large pine log, and, notwithstanding the storm, cooked and heartily enjoyed a most delicious supper; and, at the usual hour, were much more sweetly reposing than the uneasy tenant of many a curtained bed of down.

In the morning the ground was slightly covered with snow, and the storm had ceased. I could hardly realize that we were at night to leave our traveling habitation;—it seemed a matter of course, each day, to continue our journey *ad infinitum*. It is related of General Taylor that, spending a night with a friend, he abandoned his bed, and slept upon the porch. I really began to feel that a regular bed, in a regular bed-room, in a regular house, would give me the nightmare. One more camp breakfast and dinner, and we were to be once more housed like civilized beings.

The man who brought us the oats and luxuries advised the Captain to take the road through Parley's Cañon, instead of the usual emigrant road. We accordingly diverged to the left, in a few miles from our camping ground, and followed down the course of a swift mountain stream; this led us into a gorge, which exceeded in wildness anything I had yet seen. At some points the pass was so narrow, that we traveled directly in the bed of the stream—I am sure we crossed it a score of times—and why we did not break down a dozen times, and why the mules did not break their legs, is entirely past my com- prehension. The lower part of this pass was lined with rocks, fearfully high. We finally turned a sharp angle of the rocky strata, and the valley burst upon our view. The mellow light of an Indian summer sun, gave a peculiar, mild, and soft brilliancy to the whole scene. Before us was Antelope Island, rising from the bosom of the lake into a mountain; and, further south, was a mountain range, a little less lofty than that through which we had just emerged, the tops of which were covered with snow.

We had not traveled far from the mouth of the cañon, before Capt. Phelps pointed to the right, and cried out—"There is the city." What a singular spectacle! We beheld what seemed a thickly-settled neighborhood, apparently about a mile distant from us, composed of low, lead-colored dwellings, with a single white building occupying a prominent position: no steeples, minarets, or cupolas! Could that really be the Mormon capital? Was that to constitute our home for the next six months? Our party were in high spirits; and the very animals seemed animated with a premonition of approaching rest.

I cannot forget my sensations while thus approaching the termination of our weary journey: hope and fear were strangely mingled. What had the future in store for us while sojourning in this strange region, and among a strange people? Would we be kindly received, or subject to distrust, treachery, espionage, and vexation? As the thoughts of friends and home in the vast distance came crowding in, with the conviction that we were really in a prison-house of mountains, as unscalable in the winter as the clouds, my boasted courage, which had so bravely kept up during the long and weary travel, gave way. We wound our way slowly along into the city, which we reached just at evening; and it was with a most heavy heart that I was ushered into Mrs. Farnham's tasteful cottage, as our future home.

We were expected guests. Mrs. Farnham smilingly met us at the door; a bright fire was blazing upon the hearth; the supper-table was already waiting for us, spread with the same neatness and bountiful provision as in civilized lands; and, in brief time, the Arab life of our journey was exchanged for the tidy parlor and bed-room, which are to constitute our quarters for the winter. I was most agreeably surprised—I had looked only for the rude accommodations of border life.

Soon after, Judge Snow, a resident Mormon,

called to greet us on our safe arrival, and made himself very sociable. He has been here a year, and is one of the United States Judges. I inferred from a part of his conversation that polygamy does actually exist here, and that he was in favor of it. It was an incidental remark, made in reference to the right of the general government to control the local legislation of the Territories. He scanned us closely, to see, as I conjectured, how we felt on these points, and I internally laughed at the impenetrable coat of non-committalism with which Mr. F. clothed himself.

Judge Shaver also made his appearance a little later in the evening. Like ourselves, he was a new comer, having just arrived in the stage. From him we learned that Judge Reed, the Chief Justice, had started with him; but, for some reason, had become discouraged, and returned after coming as far as Fort Kearney— a circumstance we deeply regretted, as a great loss to our society. Altogether, our first evening in Utah passed off pleasantly.

The next morning we received from the post-office a most grateful supply of letters and papers from home. They were two months old. It seemed as though we were on another planet and had just received news from the earth. The casualties by fires, floods, explosions, and collisions, of two months' standing, are, to us, brought into the proximity of a single day, and create the impression that the far-off world is in a bad way. You have had time to read and forget one, before receiving intelligence of another.

We are delighted with our quarters. It is a pretty cottage, built of adobe bricks—the universal building material here; the grounds around are neatly arranged, and we are cheered with some beautiful late flowers. On the north and east we look out on the range of mountains through which we made our way into the valley; on the south the view stretches a great distance—some thirty or forty miles, they tell me—between this same range and another, which is on the western side—both covered with snow. From our west window we look out upon Antelope Island in the lake, which Mrs. Farnham says is twenty-two miles off, although it does not seem one quarter the distance. The valley, you will see, is therefore very broad; and, from this point, looks as though completely hemmed in by the mountains.

We are pleased with our landlady, who is an active, kind, and lady-like New Englander; and I have made up my mind that I can survive the winter. You will, doubtless, laugh at the facility with which I have jumped to a conclusion in this matter; and will expect me to sing a different tune by and by, when Mrs. Farnham has become sufficiently accustomed to us to exhibit the rough edges of her disposition. But recollect my female society, for the last two months, has been very limited, and and you will scarcely wonder that she seems a paragon at present. I am very sure the extreme neatness of her house could not have been gotten up merely for the occasion of our reception—there must be something real here, certainly.

We have now been four days domesticated in our new home, and our late wandering life seems almost like a dream. When I look back upon the journey, I find that, like most of the

5

incidents of human life, it has been checkered
with good and evil. My own health has been
good throughout; but the sickness of Mr. F.
was a sad drawback. He had the chills and
fever, off and on, all the way through; and
at times became so weak he could scarcely
stand. On two occasions he rode the whole
day stretched helplessly upon the bed. Of
course I had my gloomy forebodings, besides
being deprived of any little side-way excursions
to look at curious objects, from which both
had anticipated much pleasure. During the
latter part of the route he became decidedly
better.

I had anticipated very indifferent fare, and
some privation upon so long a road—but in
this was entirely disappointed. We, in fact,
lived remarkably well. In the region of the
prairie chicken, we absolutely tired of that
delicate fowl; and we had buffalo meat for
some time after we lost sight of the animal—
the extreme dryness of the atmosphere enabling
us to carry it for more than a week perfectly
sweet. After this our Mexican, José, kept us
supplied a portion of the time with antelope,

which is very much like our venison. Our
fare was often varied; and you would be
amused at the odd fashion in which some of
our messes were cooked. Among the many
things forced upon us by our never-to-be-for-
gotten friends at Fort Kearney, were a few
beans. I thought at the time they would
prove more burdensome than useful, but the
result proved otherwise. As we tired of other
things, Morse thought of the beans, and determined on bean soup. Every house-keeper
knows that this vegetable takes a great while
to cook; but our indefatigable man Friday
cooked them by installments;—he would commence them at one camp-fire, carry them along
in a tightly-covered camp-kettle to the next,
and there finish them. They proved a luxury;
and we almost literally verified the old song—

"Bean porridge hot, bean porridge cold;
  Bean porridge in the pot, nine days old."

Once we got cheated of our soup. The kettle of half-cooked beans was hung under the
carriage, and, in fording the Platte, was filled
with its turbid waters; and I laugh now when

I think of the blank dismay exhibited by Morse when he discovered the utter ruin of his mess.

I managed to play the fine lady throughout, except that, on two occasions, I mixed the short cake, when Denton and Morse had too much on hand. I was, therefore, able to read and write almost every day—the port-folio, and sometimes a cushion, serving for a table. The few books we brought with us proved a real treasure.

The men were the roughest of the rough; and, as a general rule, out-Heroded Herod in profanity. There were a few exceptions in regard to swearing, which was the more re-marked from the contrast—our own men respected our feelings on this point. Without a single exception, these rough men treated us with courtesy—and, in many instances, the very roughest manifested real kindness. José was usually quiet, and uniformly kind.

Mr. F. has called upon the Governor, and says that his reception was all he could wish. In my next I shall be able to give you some insight into Mormon society.

LETTER VIII.

WE have now had a month's experience of Mormon life. So far, we have been treated with kindness—our landlady improves on further acquaintance—we have access to a well-selected public library. Mr. Livingston, a Gentile merchant, has politely given us the freedom of some choice books, left in his possession by the late Secretary Harris. Among them are a few standard works of fiction—real treasures—and we are hoping to pass the period of our imprisonment agreeably. Yet I fear, with all these appliances, the coming winter is destined to be a tedious one. There is an oppressive sense of seclusion from the active, moving world outside of the Great Basin. The daily news, which has heretofore absorbed so much of our attention, is entirely wanting, and there seems to be but little for us to do except to watch the curious little world, in the midst of which our present fortunes are cast.

We have made one disagreeable discovery. Polygamy is not only practiced, but openly justified and advocated on religious grounds. We had some rumors of this on the way; but Mr. F. strenuously contended, that it was one of the thousand reports, circulated to the prejudice of the Mormons, by their enemies. I am afraid the other nine hundred and ninety-nine stories will prove to be true. It seems that it was practiced secretly by most of the leaders before they left the States, in obedience to a revelation of their pretended prophet, Smith; but more openly after they came here, and that, finally, during the last summer, they threw off the mask, and preached openly in favor of it, and published the sermons and pretended revelation in their newspaper. Before this period, their missionaries were instructed to deny that any such vile institution existed among them, an injunction which they readily obeyed.

We are unquestionably in the midst of a society of fanatics, who are controlled by a gang of licentious villains, and it will require all our circumspection to get along smoothly. One of our Gentile friends told Mr. F., the other day, that he would see things that would disgust him, and expressed a regret that he had brought his wife with him. These things annoy me somewhat, but I do not think they will dare resort to any lawless measures towards us.

That we are closely watched I am well persuaded. The very day after we arrived, while wholly absorbed in reading the news from home, I was suddenly startled by a pair of eyes glaring in at the west window, belonging to a malignant looking man, who was engaged in training some vines on that side of the house. Of course he desisted when he found himself observed, but I detected him, afterwards, repeating the same thing in a very furtive manner. If this man has not committed murder, it has been for want of opportunity. I have since learned that he lives but a short distance from us, upon the same lot, in a long, low, underground log hut, covered with thatch and earth, giving it very much the appearance of an ice-house. He had been employed, it seems, for a few days, to assist Father Lee, in preparing the garden and flower-bed for winter.

And who is Father Lee? Father Lee is a domestic of all work in the family, whose age precludes the idea of hard work, and whose countenance indicates a large degree of simple good. This man has left wife and children in "*Old Hingland*," for salvation's sake, that he might be in the very citadel of Zion at the consummation of all earthly things.

Mrs. Farnham is a good Mormon in all points, except that she is bitterly opposed to polygamy. But this may be only pretense to render us unguarded. She may, after all, be as much a spy upon us as the cut-throat who gazed in at the window. The fact is, we are becoming excessively suspicious. A few of the Gentile residents have called upon us, and I observe, when the subject of Mormonism is broached, they immediately lower their voices, and look around, as if apprehensive that some one may be listening at the door or windows. This is hint enough, and we have schooled ourselves, thus early, to talk in whispers. This constraint produces a sort of straight jacket sensation, from which I would gladly be relieved. I can readily see how easy it would be to get into collision with these people.

I do not know whether I have explained what is understood by "*Gentile*." The Mormons call themselves *saints* par excellence, and all others Gentiles—we are Gentiles—all are Gentiles who do not belong to this strange community of saints.

On the opposite side of the way, directly west of us, in a small adobe house, resides Phineas Young—a brother of the governor, familiarly known, however, by the uncomplimentary designation of "Old Phin." This man called, soon after our arrival, and manifested a disposition to treat us with civility. I learned from Mrs. Farnham that he had had some seven or eight wives; that his first, or real wife, still lives in the States; and that the others had all left him but one. Whether he had been reduced to this low number by necessity or inclination, I do not know. I

5*

further learned that the present Mrs. Phin desired to make my acquaintance, so an evening was appointed, and they both called. We found him very sociable, with much general information, and full of anecdote of the roving life to which all the Mormons have been, more or less, subjected. He had a great deal to say of Gentile persecutions—a theme which I find them ready enough to talk about. Among other things he gave us a history of the privations to which those saints were subject, who were the pioneers in the valley.

It seems they were driven nearly to the point of starvation, and had to dig *Sego* roots —a root extensively used by the Indians, from which they have received the name of Diggers. He gave quite a graphic description of the destruction which threatened their first crops, by the ravages of an ugly cricket, until the ravagers were in turn destroyed by flocks of white gulls, which came over the mountain tops—a thing which, he assured us, had never before been seen. Mr. F. asked him where they came from. That, he said, was a mystery—he did not doubt they were created for the occasion. The man is a Jesuit, after all. While marveling about these mysterious gulls, I could see him slyly watching the effect the narrative might have upon his audience.

I found time to have some side chat with Mrs. Phin; and learned she had been previously married to a man by the name of Canfield, and that *she had persuaded* him to take her sister, to whom she was much attached, as his second wife, thinking they could get along harmoniously. Canfield finally concluded that two were not enough, and took in a third, and then abused the two sisters. He then went off to California, searching for gold, and came back empty-handed; upon which she left him, and took refuge under the shadow of "Old Phin." Such is the substance of the story told by the woman herself; leaving discreetly untold, no doubt, the most salient points of her history. They left, pressingly inviting a return of the visit; but I internally resolved that a convenient head-ache, or something equally cogent, should always interfere.

On the corner diagonal to us, is a bright spot in this wilderness of moral darkness: an

English cabinet-maker, opposed to polygamy —a Gladdenite—and, withal, a proscribed man. What is meant by Gladdenite I do not distinctly understand, except that it designates a heresy among the saints; and this man is spoken of with a good deal of bitterness.

Directly opposite, on the north, resides Brother Wakeman, an exemplary Mormon of two wives and a host of children. He lives in a well built adobe house; but there is around the establishment an appearance of utter shiftlessness—the broken windows are stuffed with rags; the doorway and steps look as though one might stick fast in trying to pass them, and the street fences are half down. Scarce a day passes which does not exhibit some evidence of internal commotion, like a volcanic eruption, in this domicile, in one form or another. At one time three or four of the children, and one of the mothers, will be seen hurrying out, followed by the worthy brother, in hot pursuit, with threatening gestures and high voices, from the screaming treble of the youngsters to the harsh bass of the sire. At another time a number of children will stream

forth, pursued by one of the women, flourishing a broomstick. This Wakeman occasionally
comes over the way to borrow something of
Mrs. Farnham, and I get a nearer view of him.
He has a fierce, gray eye, and very florid
complexion; and looks like one of your crank
men, who are continually on the look out
for an intrusion upon their rights.

If rumor speak truly, he had warm work,
when he took in his second wife. It seems
that it is a great point with these bashaws
to procure the consent of the first wife to the
second marriage; and Brother Wakeman's wife
proving contumacious, he resorted to choking
and beating to such a degree, that the neighbors had to interfere. Really, if there was
ever a human den, where Pandemonium was
fairly incarnated and ultimated upon earth,
we have discovered it in this hopeful establishment.

One of the boys, by the name of Alma,
we have taken a kind of odd fancy to, in
spite of his rags, tricks, and dirt. He makes
a fair errand-boy, with the immediate prospect
of reward before him. He is all eyes and

mouth—looks as eagerly hungry as a young wolf—and is, withal, good-humored. He said to me, one day: "Oh, I'm mortal hungry; I reckon I shall have to go and get sego." Of course, it was difficult to resist such an appeal, which the rascal well understood. He often comes in, and our landlady rates him soundly; but I find it generally ends in giving the poor urchin something to eat.

After we had got comfortably settled in our new home, I called on Mrs. Phelps, my *compagnon du voyage*. They have taken up their quarters in the family of Major Horton, who lives two miles from here, in the northern part of the town. In going there I walked till fairly tired out, when I had the good fortune to meet Capt. Phelps in a carriage, who instantly turned about, and easily persuaded me to ride the rest of the way. He was accompanied by an intelligent-looking man, who manifested much gratification at our arrival in the city, and ventured to prophecy that we would like it so well as to make it our permanent home. I found Major Horton's a very comfortably furnished adobe dwelling, of two stories—an unusual height here, on account of the high winds from the cañons. Mrs. H. appeared lady-like; and the daughter, who is quite pretty, is a great belle among the saints.

On my way back I sauntered leisurely, and gratified my curiosity by peeping into doors and windows. The mass of the dwellings are small, low, and hut-like, and generally a little back from the street. Some of them literally swarmed with women and children; and had an aspect of extreme want of neatness. The streets and sidewalks are very broad. One thing is peculiar; at nearly every street-crossing, is a little stream of water, pebbly, clear, and sparkling, with usually a plank for the foot-passenger. These little streams have been conducted from a mountain creek of some size, for the purpose of watering the city. I have discovered, thus early, that little deference is paid to women; repeatedly, in my long walk to our boarding-house, I was obliged to retreat back from these crossing places, and stand on one side for men to cross over. There are said to be a great many of the lower order of English here; and this rudeness, so

unusual with our countrymen, may proceed
from them ; but, I suspect it to be one of the
effects of polygamy—the tendency of which
must be to bring women into a certain degree
of contempt.

The city is seated on a handsome slope,
formed by an elbow of the mountain range.
The Governor's house, which I passed in this
long walk, is at the northern side, on the first
step, or bench of the mountain, and, consequently, occupies about the highest point,
overlooking nearly the whole town—the view
extending off south, between elevated ranges.
In a prospect presenting so much that is grand
and beautiful, it seems incongruous that the
inhabitants should be in a state of degradation. I also passed the Tabernacle, Council-
house, and Tithing-office, on the same street.
These make up the public buildings, which,
in any other place, would attract but slight
attention—except, perhaps, the Tabernacle—
where their religious services are performed,
and which is peculiar from its entire want
of architectural taste or beauty. It is very
large on the ground, and has a wretchedly

tame appearance, like an immense oblong box;
but it accommodates a great audience, and is
not fairly a subject for criticism, as it was
merely built for temporary purposes. The
block on which it stands, is being surrounded
by a wall of handsomely-dressed stone; and
they talk of building a magnificent Temple
to take the place of the Tabernacle.

I was rejoiced to get back to our room,
which begins to seem home-like. We are really very comfortably situated—our room is
separated from the rest of the house by a
hall, which cuts off the noise of the family,
and Mrs. Farnham is careful to prevent us
from being annoyed by the children. Her
husband started on a mission to Australia, a
few days before our arrival, and she is now
the head of the family. She is a veritable
Yankee housekeeper, active and managing—
her table is exquisitely neat, and provided
with the best. Such butter we never tasted
before—it has a peculiar sweetness derived
from the bunch-grass, which is not to be found
in the States.

Mr. F. has made our room his office—a very

pleasant arrangement for me, as it saves me from being left alone during the day; and I am in a fair way of becoming acquainted with all the dignitaries of the Mormon empire, who come in on business or ceremony. After any one has been in, I take pains to inquire into his history, and especially whether he has more than one wife. These extra wives are known by sundry designations—some call them "*spirituals*," others, "*sealed ones;*" our landlady is fond of calling them "*fixins*," and the tone in which she brings it out is in the last degree contemptuous, and makes me laugh every time I hear it. It seems these left-hand marriages are termed *sealings;* the woman is said to be *sealed* to the man—a term in Mormon theology, of which I do not yet understand the application: nor do I yet know what is meant by "*spirituals*."

A man by the name of Wells, who was until lately the Private Secretary of the Governor, has called a number of times to urge the payment of certain claims that Mr. F. is not willing to allow. He has a cast in one eye which gives him a sinister look; and, after I learned that he had six wives, all living in common in one house, like so many brutes, the man looked perfectly hideous to me. I was amused at the persuasive and seductive manner in which he urged payment—contending that the Government would not allow their officer to suffer, even if it was not strictly according to law; and when this did not make the desired impression, he manifested some angry impatience, which, of course, only made matters worse. One evening Mr. F. drew him into conversation in regard to the settlement of the Territory by the Mormons, and notwithstanding my strong dislike, I could not help being interested in his account of their troubles with the "*Utes*," as the Indians around here are called. Wells, it seems, acted as the leader of the saints in this Indian war. They came to an open rupture with these miserable natives in the winter of 1850, and killed some of them in various skirmishes. He said it was very similar to chasing wild beasts, and that they would often stumble upon the poor creatures while burrowed, as it were, in the thick grass, and concealed in clumps of willows. They captured quite a number of squaws and children, and provided for them till spring—some of the squaws, however, stole away and lay in the hot-spring lake, near the city, to keep warm—just keeping their heads out of water, and in this condition they would catch the wild fowl swimming around them and devour them raw.

A man by the name of Clawson came in with Wells a number of times. One of our Gentile visitors enlightened us in regard to him. After being married about two years, he had taken in, for his second wife, a girl by the name of Judd. This was accomplished by a regular courtship, carried on with all the little attentions and deference usually paid by love-stricken swains; but, during this process, his young wife would often be detected, at their convivial assemblies, weeping most bitterly. Punishment will no doubt come in due season; but justice, in this instance, seems amazingly slow. I would have it swift and terrible.

In addition to these calls from the masculine portion of the community, which promise to be of so much interest, our boarding-house is a frequent resort for some of the poor "*spirituals*," to whom Mrs. Farnham furnishes little odd jobs, to enable them to eke out a scanty living. I have already managed to obtain from one of these miserable creatures a sad picture of the state of affairs in her household. There are three wives in the family, who being in a regular strife for the mastery, and having no common interest, everything is out of joint. At first I found it difficult to approach her, but, by a little tact, I overcame her reserve; and the fount once unsealed, she poured forth her troubles. She is a wretched specimen of a woman—poorly dressed, poorly fed, and exhibits a sense of degradation. In this particular case, the first wife had revenged herself to some extent, by managing to make drudges of the other two.

I must not forget to mention, that a man called soon after our arrival, and introduced himself as a Mr. Colborn, from Cayuga county, in New York, and said his wife was one of the Ozmuns in Tompkins county. We were, of course, pleased to see a man from so near home—he seemed almost like an acquaintance. He appears very simple, complained much of poverty and sickness, and my sympathies were strongly excited for him.

Among the physical curiosities of this wonderful region are two thermal springs—one called the "hot spring," about three miles from the northern limits of the city—and the "warm spring," two and a half miles nearer. This latter they have conducted in pipes to a bathing-house, to which we paid a visit one day last week.   The building is large, and originally intended for a hotel; but as the emigrants to California and Oregon, from which its principal patronage was to be derived, came into the city on the eastern and southern side, they were caught up by private boarding-houses, and it has fallen into decay.

We found it very much dilapidated—the doors from their hinges, and the tubs leaking—and it was even difficult to secure the necessary privacy. A part of the house was occupied by a family, or, rather, by two families, for there was a father with two wives, and his son with two more.   On entering

their room to get access to the baths, I observed the elder of the two men looked very
much crippled. I questioned him like a true
Yankee, and found that he had been a sufferer
at Nauvoo. In talking about it, he manifested
such a vindictive and savage spirit against the
Gentiles, that I should be afraid to meet him
alone, and was glad to put an end to the
colloquy. A good-natured young woman,
with a baby in her arms, waited upon me.
She proved to be one of the wives of the
young man; and by further inquiry, I drew
forth that they had both been married to him
at the same time, so that neither could claim
the precedence. You will ask whether such
things can be? Yes, they can be with just
such women. She was one of those good-
natured, stupid fools, that would gulp down
the most preposterous proposition, merely
saying, perhaps, *"Du tell!"* or *"You don't say
so!"* or making some similar remark. I am
quite ready to conclude that a large portion
of female Mormonism is made up of similar
materials.

After fairly getting into the water, I found

the bathing delightful. The temperature must have been as high as one hundred, and the water was very dense and perfectly clear. We walked some distance further to the spring itself, at the foot of the mountain, and found an immense rush of water, forming large pools by the side of the road, and smoking as if ready to boil; and the ground was coated with the salts with which the water is impregnated. An Irishman was there with one foot in the current which gurgled from the fountain, trying to cure some real or imaginary evil. Like most Paddies, he gave us a copious flood of the brogue. He recounted over the many virtues of the spring, making it fully equal to the blarney stone of ould Ireland, and among other things, he said, "the likes of it for soup was unknownst intirely, because it gave such an illigant flavor." This is the only Irish specimen we have seen, and, as we are told there are very few in the valley, we hope to meet him again.

Day before yesterday, Mr. F. received a note from the Governor, requesting him to come and see him on business relating to the

Legislative Assembly, which is to meet early next month; and apologized for not calling, himself, on the ground of illness. He went, as requested, to the Governor's house, and found him crouching over the fire, with his cloak and hat on, complaining of "mountain fever." After a little time, Mrs. Young (the *real* Mrs. Young) came in, and was introduced, and appeared agreeable and conversable. Among other things, she expressed a wish to call on me, which was, of course, duly responded to. So I am to receive a call from the Governor's lady before calling on her, and this relieves me on a point of etiquette, about which I was somewhat perplexed.

6

LETTER IX.

GREAT SALT LAKE CITY, Dec., 1852.

ANOTHER month has brought us into more intimate acquaintance with Mormon society, which we find has two faces—one for the Gentiles and the other for the saints. It will not do here to judge from appearances. A man stopping here for a few days, or even weeks, would be very apt to go away impressed with the idea that it was a prosperous and happy community. He finds a city which has been built up within a brief period; he sees a certain degree of commendable industry; he hears the saints addressing each other as brothers and sisters, seeming to live together in great harmony; and pursues his journey to California or Oregon, without obtaining a glimpse of the "dead men's bones and rottenness" which lie festering beneath this whited sepulchre. The brief sojourner is so much surprised at what he sees and hears, that he writes a long letter to one of the New York journals, in which he depicts, in glowing colors, the prosperity and happiness of the saints; and, what is still more wonderful, he makes the discovery, that polygamy has been found to be compatible with domestic harmony.

A closer scrutiny, and, perhaps I may with propriety add, certain facilities, which a man cannot command, is necessary to penetrate the veil that conceals the true deformity of Mormonism from the world. A singular incident bids fair to give us a view of the very bottom of this sink of pollution. Some few weeks after our arrival, a man from Westchester County, N. Y., and who has relatives in our county, called to see us. He was a zealous saint, proved to be an incessant talker, and poured forth a wordy harangue in favor of his system. We marveled at the object of so much noisy rant in so small a congregation; but the secret came out at the close of the interview. It seems that some one, whose name he did not mention, had written to him, that we were both good subjects for conversion, and this was the first installment of the effort in that direction. Mr. F. allowed this proselyting spirit to go away in the full belief that he had made a favorable impression, and was, a few days after, told by one of the Gentiles, that we were regarded as almost on the anxious seat.

This effort has been followed up by a very singular genius in petticoats, who promises to be an unfailing and infallible source of information on all points. Her name is Shearer, and she is familiarly known as "Aunty Shearer." She is, in every respect, a unique specimen of womanhood—tall, stout, bony, square-cornered—with cold, yet eager gray eyes, great volubility, and grim aspect. If she had remained in the States, under certain associations, she would have blossomed out early, as a Woman's Rights champion, or one of the "strong-minded," who have a mission to reform this wicked age. On most points, except that of the Mormon superstition, her ignorance is gross, like darkness; so thick that you can cut it with a knife and dull the edge. She lives hard by, on the next block west, and is a frequent visitor at our boarding-house. Well, this queer specimen of severe angularity of mind and body thinks me a good subject; and I have found a treasure, or rather a convenient forcing-pump, which yields to every motion of the handle.

She was an early disciple, and I have gathered enough of her history to understand that the prophet, Joseph Smith, completely robbed her, under various plausible pretenses, of her little property, which, of course, was in the line of *his* particular mission; and after keeping her for a time in his family as a sort of domestic drudge, the rogue shipped her off, by a revelation, to sustain herself the best way she could. She has great industry, and struggled bravely through all the troubles of these pseudo saints, and finally floated along in the current of emigration to Salt Lake; and is now gaining a living as a nurse, and, of course, knows all that is going on. It seems she has a husband wandering somewhere about the earth, but his heart proving too hard to be softened by Mormon influence, or from some other cause, she has abandoned him to his fate. On this point, she manifests some reserve. She bears his name, to be sure, but his existence and whereabouts are mysteries which my profane curiosity has not been permitted fully to penetrate. It is quite probable "thereby hangs a tale." Perhaps this mythic Mr. Shearer may turn up before we leave the valley, or else altogether evaporate.

Polygamy has been a great stumbling block to Aunty Shearer—it was promulgated, however, by the immaculate Joseph, and she has managed to choke it down with a wry face. She is disposed to conceal its effects, and would, if her shrewdness was equal to her zeal; but she has a natural love of gossip, which will find vent in spite of all other considerations. I can always tell when some precious item, in that important branch of saintly domesticity, lies heavy upon her conscience, and have no difficulty in relieving her of the burden. I tell her this is a point very difficult for us to get over. She says, it is not compulsory, and if we join, my husband need not take another wife.

In the early part of the month, one of the

twelve Apostles, Lorenzo Snow, a small, neatly-
dressed, dapper-looking man, called on business, in relation to some improvements they
desire to make in their Legislative Assembly
room. He was accompanied by a tall six-
footer, by the name of Cumming, with, to
me, a very forbidding countenance. The one
looked as if he never did anything wrong—
the other, as if he never did anything else.
They put on their best manner; and, as their
wishes were likely to be complied with, entered
readily into general conversation. This Snow,
it seems, had lately returned from Europe,
spending some time in Italy, the particular
field of his efforts, and gave us, in an agreeable manner, much interesting information in
reference to the lower classes in that country.
He appeared to have some enlarged views, in
regard to the development of the agricultural
and mineral resources of the Territory, and
of the importance of the city we were in, as
a half-way house between the East and West.
He had a funny way of puckering his mouth
in conversation, which I attributed to a feeling
of importance derived from his apostleship;

yet he exhibited more polish than any we had seen here, and we were pleased with him. We flattered ourselves that we had found at least one man of sufficient taste and refinement, to say nothing of moral principle, to be free from the degradation of polygamy; but it is not always safe to judge from appearances.

At the first opportunity, I applied to my Mormon dictionary, Aunty Shearer, and was duly enlightened with regard to Elder Snow. He resides near us, in the second house beyond Brother Wakeman's, with six wives, in two little huts, and has twelve children. In the principal hut, the real wife sits at the head of the table, and pours out tea and coffee for the rest of the bevy. The latest acquisition to this highly-favored household, and, of course, the reigning sultana for the time, was the only one of them with whom he condescended to correspond during his absence. Her education, however, had not attained the dignity of an ability to read, and, either because the other inmates of the harem were in like predicament, or that she was unwilling they should see these loving epistles, she took them to the neighbors to be translated. Like all other Mormon missionaries, he was a beggar; and the story is, that he has been so successful in his mendicity, that the cottages are to give place to a large adobe mansion, which will make a more convenient seraglio.

Such is Elder Snow; and yet he could talk about the works of art in Rome and Paris, with some apparent appreciation of their beauties. Like our other visitors, he expressed a wish that our sojourn might be rendered agreeable, but not a word of invitation to visit his family, or that his *wife* would be happy to see me, which usually forms so pleasant a finale to an agreeable interview. These are interdicted subjects to them all; nor is it strange. These miserable creatures have houses where they stay, and a discordant and disunited association of women and children, but no *families*—there are none of the comforts and delights of home with the polygamist.

It has been a matter of great wonder to me how the women could be induced to consent to polygamous marriages. It is so re-

6*

pugnant to all the instincts and feelings of a true woman, that I could not understand it. The mystery is partly solved. It seems that one part of their ridiculous creed is, that a woman cannot be saved, unless she is sealed or married to a Mormon; and he must be one, too, who will remain steadfast to the end; and, as they are noted for a great number of apostates, it becomes an object with these silly fools to get into the harems of the priests and elders, because it is believed they will not apostatize. Of course, any one with half an eye can see the object of the prophet Smith, in promulgating such a doctrine; and the wonder is, that its transparency is not obvious to all.

I made this discovery by talking with Aunty Shearer, about an old lady by the name of Western—commonly known as "Mother Western"—one of Brigham's wives. I was marveling why she should marry in her old age, especially as fiftieth or sixtieth wife, when my oracle said "she was only sealed for the sake of salvation." She further informed me that Brigham had more wives in this way than anybody knew of—that he did not even know himself, the sealing to him being considered a more certain guarantee for salvation, because he was the reigning prophet, and was sure to remain faithful.

One scarcely knows whether to be amazed most at the profane profligacy of the leaders, or the superstitious credulity of their dupes. The effect of the Mormon creed is, evidently, to gather together a low class of villains, and a still lower class of dupes; and it follows that the latter are easily governed. The only disturbing element is, that the villains may quarrel among themselves; and, so far as I can learn, this has happened on more than one occasion. A further effect will, probably, be, to operate as a Botany Bay to society generally, by relieving it of its superabundance of both classes.

We were awakened on Christmas morning by hearing familiar airs from a brass band parading around in an open carriage. They began thus early to usher in a merry Christmas, by serenading the dignitaries of the Mormon church. Brigham first, then Kimball and

Dr. Richards, and after that the twelve apostles; and, last of all, bashaws of lesser note. Father John Smith was also complimented, and gave the serenaders his paternal blessing. We, poor insignificant Gentiles, chanced to obtain a trifle of benefit from this traveling concert as they passed along our street.

The old song says, "Christmas comes but one a year"—but where is ours? Where to us the glories of Santa Claus—the reunion and merry greetings of friends—"the sound of the church-going bell"—the cheerful "feast of reason and flow of soul?" They are not here—they belong to another world—they are embalmed in the memory of things that are past—they live in the anticipations of the future.

The little Farnhams have their enjoyments, and are as gleeful over the donations of Criss Cringle as all other juveniles: and the mother, too, does her share. She has loaded her dinner-table with all kinds of game, brandt, canvas-back duck, antelope, hare, and intended to have served up a sirloin of grisly bear, but bruin wisely managed to evade his human foe;

and we certainly are well satisfied to dispense with any further addition to the good cheer.

I have been amusing myself this afternoon, with the crowd returning from the Tabernacle. Here is a man passing with four women, all lovingly locking arms. The male animal is in the centre, and the two that were sealed lately, as I am assured by Aunty Shearer, are nearest to his person—the other two are outsiders. The brides are bedizened with some finery; but all look poorly clothed for the season. As a general rule, the mass of the foreigners do not have the comfortable appearance of our Irish women with their blanket shawls. The Welch, Swedes, and Danes, had such glowing accounts of the fineness of the climate, that their winter clothing was laid aside before crossing the plains.

On the other side of the way is a man with three spirituals: he is in advance, and the women are following in single file—the extreme rear is, probably, his first wife. This man evidently acts out his principles. I saw them going to the Tabernacle in the same order.

Single couples are also in the throng, mostly

foreigners; to be distinguished by their dress, and a less sad and more hopeful expression on the part of the females, especially those who belong to the emigration of the present year. On this side of the street is an intelligent, gentlemanly-looking man, with his wife and three children, gazing at the strange people as they pass. They stop and look at Mrs. Farnham's flower garden, while the children are jumping back and forth over the clear stream which runs by our door.

There comes Father Lee in his steeple-crowned hat and cloak, the cast-off habiliments of one of the Gentile boarders, and of somewhat too ample proportions for his diminutive figure. His very countenance shines with the unction he has received, and I cannot resist the temptation to go into the kitchen, and obtain from him a rehearsal while eating his dinner. If Gabriel himself, in bright effulgence, and with "sonorous metal blowing martial sounds," had descended in person, the effect could not have aroused the old simpleton more effectually than the preaching he had heard. In the rambling and blasphemous discourse which Brigham had delivered, was a strong admonition to the dilatory to add to their kingdoms by taking wives, inasmuch as the saints would soon have to fight with the Gentiles, for the possession of Zion in the tops of the mountains. I could almost see the satanic leer he must have cast around, to witness the effect of this announcement upon the crowd of dupes before him.

If they were all like Father Lee, his efforts to keep them in subjection would be light, indeed. The mild brown eyes of the simple old man light up, with a kind of child-like animation, in recounting what he has heard, and I almost feel guilty in quizzing him. But what a dull time I should have of it without some such resource. Seeing my apparent anxiety to be refreshed by a few drops from this precious sanctuary, he broke out with—

"Oh! *sister*, how I do pray that you will be brought into Zion, and never more go back into the wicked world!"

And then, to give effect to this exhortation, he went on to speak of the miraculous things that had happened to him while preaching in

the streets of London—how, many and many
a time, bricks and other ugly missiles flew
around him like hailstones, and had been di-
verted from his valuable brains so marvelously,
that his persecutors had been struck dumb, as
in the times of the Apostles.

It seems he knew nothing of spiritual wifery
before he came here. I suggested to him that,
after such a discourse from Brigham, he was
in duty bound to take two or three wives,
at least. He said he knew such was his duty,
and thought he would when his prospects
brightened a little. Now the dormitory of
this old creature is a covered wagon, near the
kitchen door, from which he emerges, in the
cold morning, looking like a dormouse, just
awakened from a winter's nap—and this rare
privilege is accorded to him as a matter of
grace. Not much room is there for even
one wife, and his kingdom will not soon am-
plify, if he depends on the increase of his
worldly goods.

Father Lee is a good type of one of the
elements of Mormonism—the most unbounded
credulity—easily persuaded to perform as a

duty that which, in civilized lands, would consign the perpetrator to the penitentiary or the
scaffold. To look at him sitting before me, he
does not seem capable of harming an insect—
but what assurance is there that he would not
put arsenic or strychnine in my food, if told by
the Prophet that it was his duty to destroy an
enemy of the true faith?

Dec. 29. Among our agreeable visitors must
be numbered Mr. Haywood, the United States
Marshal, and his *first* wife. They called at an
early period of our arrival, and have continued
to treat us with attentive politeness. She
is as pretty, well-informed, and accomplished
as you will find anywhere in a thousand, and
exhibits withal, what is not common here,
good taste in dress.

After forming their acquaintance, I was surprised to learn from Aunty Shearer, that he
has two other wives; one known as Sister
Very, old enough to be his mother, and who,
in fact, seems to fill that office in the family.
Of course, she was said to be "sealed for the
sake of salvation." Mrs. H. and Sister Very
called one day, and I found the latter an

agreeable, quiet, elderly lady from Old Salem, sufficiently well informed, and everything about her such as you would expect to find in a woman of her age from the land of steady habits, except in the single point of being the second of two wives in the same family.

This is the only instance in which I have seen two wives of the same man together; and, judging from appearances, the age of the one precluded anything like jealousy on the part of the other. What jarring there may be between them at home, I cannot tell. I only know that, in my presence, they treated each other with that degree of affectionate cordiality which properly belongs to the intercourse between mother and daughter. What a strange spectacle! Here was an elderly woman, apparently of fair intelligence, and correct notions of propriety, in whom the feelings and instincts of womanhood may be supposed to have become fixed and permanent habits of thought, yielding all that is valuable to a ridiculous system of imposture—in other words, becoming a concubine. I can no longer wonder that girls are so easily made fools of, when they have before them the influence of such examples. A young woman here stands alone, without the warning admonitions of parents or friends, and must yield to the universal custom, unless her own unaided strength is sufficient to save her.

If the worthy Marshal had stopped here, I could tolerate him very well, considering we are sojourners in the Mormon capital. But he has still another wife, and I learn from my universal referee, that, in the States, she was one of the "strong minded"—in fine, a pseudo-lecturer on progressivism—who was so fully persuaded that womankind were in a false position, that she has ended in making herself what she is. The Marshal keeps her and her baby on his farming establishment in Juab, about eighty miles from here. He spends six weeks of his time there, and then the same time with his family here, and so alternates between the two. To-day he has been in, partly on business and partly to make a friendly call; and I felt disposed to be hateful towards him. But he appeared so cordial and friendly, and gave us such warm and pressing invitations to visit his family, differing in this respect from the rest of these vagabonds, that he partially succeeded in disarming resentment.

He claims that he is in the performance of religious duty, and manifests the strongest appearance of sincerity. I asked him to-day if he had the same love for his wife in Juab as for his first wife. His reply was:

"It is a very singular question."

"Why so? You loved, or pretended to love your first wife at the time of your marriage."

"Certainly; and I tell my last, that when she has been tried in the furnace of affliction as Mrs. H. has, my love will be equal."

A pretty "furnace of affliction," truly, which is intended for the torment of women alone! I intimated that men ought to be scorched a little, too; but he contended that they had their share in other ways. All this was said with a degree of earnest sincerity, creating the conviction that the man may be a sincere believer in Mormonism. But alas! for his poor wife. When they called together one day, I for a moment detected in her counte-

nance, while in repose, a look so gloomily
sad, that her whole heart of agony lay bare
before me. Poor, poor, wife! Her days are
destined to be few, and full of trouble.

LETTTER X.

GREAT SALT LAKE CITY, Jan., 1853.

THE plot thickens; we are getting deeper and deeper into the merits of the subject; the Mormon mythology grows interesting. If the contents of Auburn State's prison, with females to match, cquld be isolated in a country by themselves, and induced to believe themselves a persecuted race, and that thieving and other crimes were virtues, such a community would furnish a faint counterpart of the worshipers of Beelzebub, in this secluded region. Rig up a system that will fasten itself upon the superstitious credulity and animal appetites of the stupidly ignorant, and you are ready for a flourishing business.

Jan. 5th. To-day I have had a very interesting interview with one of the new comers. I have seen her twice before, and found her so evidently intelligent, as to make it a matter for especial wonder how she could ever become a Mormon. The family consists of her husband, herself, and two children—a son and daughter; the latter about fifteen, and good looking. A fine market, truly, for a young girl!

The last time she was here, I was tempted to ask her if she was willing her husband should take another wife. Her face flushed up to her temples, and she gave me an evasive answer; but our landlady was present, and she felt under some restraint. To-day we were alone, and, after inspecting doors and windows, she has poured forth a perfect tempest of indignation at the outrages which have come to their knowledge. It seems they came, in utter ignorance of polygamy, with the view of making this place their permanent home. Mr. W. purchased a house and lot, and they are now housekeeping. He has a quantity of cattle, at present under the charge of herders, and it was his original intention to go on to California in the spring, to find a market for them, leaving his family here in the mean time. This purpose is now changed, and it is their intention to go on together in the spring, not again to return; but to effect this with as little sacrifice of property as may be, it is quite necessary to keep their own counsels.

She is a woman of masculine activity of mind, who has been very free in the expression of her thoughts, and, consequently, finds it difficult to restrain herself; but they are seriously apprehensive in regard to their ability to extricate themselves from their disagreeable predicament, and she finds it a safety valve to her feelings to converse with me. Together we are able to pass summary judgment on the wretches assembled here, and readily consign them to the very hottest part of the infernal torrid zone.

Mr. W. will be victimized to some extent. Two of the leaders managed to get into his debt a few hundred dollars. To recover what is his due, sell his house and lot, and get away unmolested, is now his anxious purpose; and if he finally escapes with the loss only of a thousand dollars, they will be satisfied.

She is a well-read hydropathist, and has been called upon repeatedly in cases of scarlet fever, now prevailing; and she gives a graphic though sad account of the sufferings of some of the poor children. One family, in which there were two wives, was living in a small hut—three children very sick—two beds and a cook-stove in the same room, creating the air of a pest house. The husband is a member of the Legislature, and is reputed to be a graduate of old Harvard, and a man of some science. On expressing solicitude for the safety of his children, she asked him how he could expect them to recover while compelled to breathe such an atmosphere; and very plainly intimated to him that his domestic habits were unfavorable to health. Of what use, however, to talk to such men?—as well ask the bacchanalian to dash away the cup, while the fiery liquid is running down his throat.

10th. Among the frequent visitors at Mrs. Farnham's is a tall and rather interesting-looking young woman, who is known by the name of Harriet Cook. She is one of Brigham's early sealed ones, by whom she has one child; is quite good-looking, and superior in point of native smartness; but exceedingly capricious

7

and variable in her feelings and conversation. The first time I saw her she seemed to have an oppressive sense of her real condition; expressed herself bitterly of her ruin, of the abominations of the harem, and even of hatred towards her child, representing it as an ugly, ungovernable little wretch. I felt much interest for her. I asked her why she did not go to California. She answered, sadly: "Here, I am as good as Mary Ann" (Brigham's first wife) "and the rest of them—but, elsewhere, I am an outcast. My brother wishes me to go, but it is of no use."

To-day this woman has called again, and I don't know when, in a conversation with one of my own sex, my disgust has been more strongly excited. She launched forth into a sort of exposé of the filthy customs of the harem, in language so coarse and vulgar, and with so much apparent gusto, that all sympathy for her is at an end, and hereafter I can only talk with her, as with some others, merely to gain information. She is a fair specimen of the utter and hopeless degradation effected by the Mormon system; and, as she grows older, will doubtless take a malignant delight in aiding to seduce others into the same unfortunate condition.

14th. Yesterday we went to the Tabernacle, for the first time, and I think my curiosity in that direction is satisfied for the season. Phineas Young acted as guide, and secured us a good seat. The throng was immense—Mr. F. says at least two thousand—and occupied seats looking down to a platform on the west side, where the high priests and elders were assembled for the services of the day.

It was a strange assemblage. If I were a scientific phrenologist, I would undertake some classification. There were a few intelligent countenances, interspersed with sly cunning and disgusting sensuality; in both male and female, a large mass of credulity, and an abundance of open-mouthed, gawky stupidity. There was no prevailing fashion; and the great variety of costume indicated a gathering from all points of the compass: some fashionable bonnets, stuck on the tip of the comb, with plenty of gauze and feathers, in close proximity to steeple crowns, with fronts big enough to hìde the beauties or deformities beneath; and these cheek by jowl with projecting fronts and cap-crowns, so unwieldy-looking that women of this fast age would find difficult navigation under them with a head wind—cloaks, casques, et cetera, to correspond.

One woman, sitting in front of us, turned around and fixed a pair of large, piercing, black eyes upon me. Her gaze manifested more than common curiosity, mingled with the expression of a grieved and unquiet spirit, trying to comprehend how a Gentile looked, whose happiness was not in the keeping of a Mormon husband. Aunty Shearer tells me she was from Springfield, Mass., well connected, has made great sacrifices to gather with the saints, and that her husband is soon to take as his second wife the daughter of a man by the name of Colborne. By-the-by, this Colborne has already made our acquaintance, on the score of being connected, by marriage, with some of our old neighbors in Tompkins County, and this circumstance may secure us an invitation to the wedding.

The principal discourse was delivered by

Parley Pratt, and was made up mostly of a rambling and disconnected glorification of the saints. As an intellectual effort, it was beneath contempt. One thing was peculiar— he resorted to the same kind of clap-trap common in political assemblages, which excited the boisterous mirth of his audience; and somehow it did not strike me as out of place in such a gathering. As to devotional feeling, there was no manifestation of it whatever. It seemed like anything else than a religious meeting; and a full band of music, stationed in front of the platform, strengthened the impression that we had come to witness some puppet-show, or other kindred performance.

17th. Last evening we went to the theatre at Social Hall, a building erected for purposes of amusement. The acting was on a dais or platform, raised some three or four feet above the room occupied by the spectators. The play was the Lady of Lyons, and the performance so much better than we anticipated, that I should have enjoyed it well enough had it not been for some side acting in the crowd, which must preclude us from going again to the same place. How thoroughly and horribly poisoned is everything in this society!

To-day Mrs. Cook called on me, who last night performed at the theatre, in the character of the mother of Claude; and performed it better, too, than you will commonly find. She is an English woman of decided intelligence, staying here through the winter with her children—her husband having gone on to California. She assures me she never before attended a theatre, either in England or America, and being, withal, an accomplished musician, she is much petted here. How could she be a Mormon? Perhaps, like Mrs. W., she is disgusted with it—or, as in the case of a great many, there may be some cogent reason, not yet told, why the society of the outside world has become unpleasant.

We learn from this lady many curious things about their theatre. Some of the actors have been on the stage before, and appear better than mere amateur performers. Among these is a Mrs. Wheelock, whose husband has gone on a mission; and, in consequence of his absence, the male actors are in full chase after her; for it seems that the fact, of a woman being already married, does not prevent her from being sealed again, provided her husband be absent. One of the most eager in this pursuit is a man who performed Claude well, in the Lady of Lyons, and is already the husband of three wives. She was so much of an attraction among the actors in this side play, as to occasionally interfere with the performance intended for the amusement of the public!

Mrs. Cook is working for bread, and complains bitterly in regard to the profits being used up by the unusual number of free tickets. Brigham, with ten or a dozen adjuncts, Kimball, with as many more, and so on through the whole gang, have to be let in free, while the performers are not allowed to bring their families without pay. Of course, where deadheads, like autumn leaves, literally cover the floor, the sum to be divided, after deducting expenses, is exceedingly small.

21st. Yesterday was so pleasant that I made another visit to the bath; and on returning took something of a detour, strolling very leisurely, and occasionally dropping into an open door to rest. I find the women very conversable. In one house was a tidy English woman, from Bath, of some native refinement of manner. The room was garnished with little mementoes of her native city; and, as she took down a print to show me the environs, and the particular point from which she came, her eyes filled with tears at the remembrance of home. I felt some hesitation in probing her heart with the ruthless question —"Are you the only wife?" Pretty soon, a broad, red-faced woman came in, and seemed perfectly at home. As soon as she went out of the room, I said :—

"That woman lives with you ?"

"Yes."

"Are you relatives ?"

The poor thing twisted her apron—her lips quivered. I then asked :—

"She is your husband's second wife ?"

It was some moments before she could find words to assure me that it was even so. She then went on to narrate, in a simple, artless way, how happily she and her husband had lived together; how they were anxious to emigrate to this country; how they had been told that the valley of Salt Lake was a paradise; that her husband could have land for nothing, and earn five dollars a day; how their expenses had been defrayed by the Mormon agents, to be refunded by her husband's labor here on the public works. And then, with tears streaming down her face, she said her husband, about three months since, had been persuaded to marry another wife, and how badly she felt when she first heard of his resolution.

This coarse, blowzy, greasy specimen of womanhood had ruled her with a rod of iron. She could not even have the privilege of a cup of tea without asking this jade's permission, so effectually had the intruder usurped all authority in this humble abode. My heart wept for her. She believed in Mormonism because her husband did; and he believed because he thought it a fine thing to be a landholder, get high wages, and be a priest in the church. This kind of logic probably

7*

accounts for the conversion of the great mass of English here.

24th. Aunty Shearer *is* a curiosity. If ever a menagerie of human beings should be gathered together by some enterprising Barnum, I now bespeak for her the post of lioness of the collection. With all her religious absurdities, she exhibits in many things a certain degree of Yankee shrewdness and thrift. She is like some of the country we have passed through, where there are a few spots fit for cultivation, in a wilderness of rocky sterility.

I have been to her place to-day, where she has her solitary lair, unless, indeed, she is secretly sealed to some one, as I tell her she may be. She looks wondrous grim at these profane suspicions, but holds her temper, merely saying—"My dear, how can you talk so ?"

Her house is a curiosity shop, of that kind of household gods and goddesses which a penny saving New Englander would be likely to treasure up—a lot of odd traps, many of which have been kept upon the principle that they may possibly come into use some time during the present generation. These valuables hail mostly from the metropolis of notions, and have escaped mob violence in Missouri and Illinois, where buildings were ruthlessly torn down over the heads of the widow and the orphan, as she pathetically relates—they were carefully garnered up at "winter quarters," in the Indian country, and have escaped all subsequent disasters by flood and field, bating, of course, some breaks, cracks, and rubs, which appear like honorable scars upon war-worn veterans.

She often walks over her acre, to be sure that she has gathered in her whole crop. An inveterate gleaner she is, but not quite realizing the sweet pictures our artists give us of Ruth and Tamar of old. I take great delight in watching her as she sallies forth at evening, on the plateau north of us, after her cow. I readily recognize her old yellow marten fur cape—her wide cap-border flapping in the wind, under a comical-looking hood—and her dress, some of her own handiwork in spinning and weaving, just wide enough and none to spare, around her gaunt form. This notable dress is

Bloomer enough to display a serviceable pair of brogans. Thus attired, and looking for all the world like a picture of Grant Thorburn in petticoats, she strides along, armed with a stout stick, bidding defiance alike to the tawny digger and the grizzly bear.

27th. Last evening we attended the Governor's party at Social Hall—an affair sufficiently unique in its way. Invitations had been given out some two weeks previously, and we were among the invited. This Social Hall is a large building, which the saints have erected for the sole purposes of parties of pleasure and theatrical performances. It is provided with a kitchen, in one part of the basement, for the preparation of the feast, on occasions like the present.

We went sufficiently late not to be among the first arrivals, and were ushered into an ante-room, to be divested of cloaks and shawls. From this, a short flight of steps brought us into a long saloon, where six cotillions were in active motion. Another short flight landed us on a raised platform, which overlooked the dancing-party, and here a band of music were in the full tide of performance. This dais was well accommodated with seats, including two or three sofas, on which were elders and apostles reclining, with a few of their concubines. Brigham was there, and had his hat on, according to his usual habit. We were treated with distinguished attention—the company generally seemed to exert themselves to make the evening pleasant to us. Our old acquaintance, Judge Snow, was there, with Mrs. S., his only wife; and I took advantage of our familiar footing with both to inquire out all the peculiarities of the evening.

Elder Kimble, one of the chief men, was present, and very sociable. He has a harem, numbering some twenty-five or thirty; but, strange to say, has continued to treat his real wife (so the story goes) as superior to the rest. She was at his right hand on the present occasion, and looked care-worn and sad; on his left was one of his sealed ones, a keen, shrewd-looking woman, from Philadelphia, and who, in the few words of conversation I had with her, evinced some intelligence. Near them sat a delicate woman, with raven hair and piercing black eyes, who proved to be Eliza Snow, the Mormon poetess, and who belongs to Brigham's harem. Polygamy cannot be a subject calculated to produce poetic inspiration—at least the effusions which appear under her name in the *Deseret News* would scare the Muses out of their senses.

I found Mrs. Orson Hyde a pleasant woman, of much simplicity of manners, and to her husband's credit be it said, he lives with her alone, although one of the twelve apostles. Another of the twelve, Amasa Lyman, was pointed out, a man of grossly sensual appearance. This man lives in San .Bernardino, and has a straggling harem, extending at convenient points from that place to Salt Lake. He collects the tithings in California, and is constantly going back and forth.

A heavy, dark-colored, beetle-browed man was pointed out as Elder John Taylor, who had been badly wounded when the prophet was murdered in Illinois. He had his wife on one arm, on the other was a young widow from Tennessee, reputed to be wealthy, and reputed also to have been lately sealed to this pious elder.

The cotillions upon the floor when we went in were soon danced out, and the dancers came crowding upon the platform—and here happened what seemed to me the crowning incident of the evening: Parley Pratt marched up with four wives, and introduced them successively as Mrs. Pratts. The thing was done with such an easy, nonchalant air, that I had difficulty in keeping from laughing outright. The thought came over me, with what scorn these people, who are here first and foremost, would be banished from society at home. Did the man do this to show what he could do, or because he thought politeness required it of him? I don't know. Some, however, only introduced the first wife, and I internally thanked them for the forbearance. One thing was peculiar—it was only the first wives that tried to make themselves familiar with me.

Dancing continued fast and furious till a late hour. Each man danced with two women at a time, and took the lead in all the chassés promenades; so it seems that even in their amusements women take a subordinate position. The private secretary of the Governor acted as master of the ceremonies; and, at the commencement of each cotillion, called off the number with which each man was furnished on entering the establishment.

The supper came off late, and I was rejoiced at the signal, for I had become tired of the scene. The feast was abundant and well got up, and we were waited upon with attention, and such was probably the case with the rest. Mrs. Snow pointed out to us numbers of the Governor's wives, who were active in waiting upon the tables. We retired soon after supper.

28th. I dropped into Aunty Shearer's this morning, and found there a bright-eyed little girl, rummaging among the curiosities of the worthy dame. She was neatly and even prettily dressed, and I correctly judged that her home had, as yet, escaped pollution from the plurality system. She belongs to an English family of a better class than is usually found here. Her father is a man of business capacity, has a subordinate post connected with the

Legislative Assembly, which does not seem to be recognized by the general government, and is in trouble about his pay. Of course I did not learn these things from the child; but, when I found to whom she belonged, and that the little thing was intelligent beyond her years, I yielded to a temptation, justifiable only from the circumstances, and questioned her freely about her family and their previous history— wishing to see how far an unsophisticated child would confirm the accounts we have of Mormon rascalities.

In what way they have been converted to Mormonism I could not learn. They had a comfortable property in England, and, as people before them had chased Jack-o'-lanterns, they, too, were induced to gather with the saints. They got into St. Louis, the usual place of rendezvous for emigrating parties, in good health and spirits, after a prosperous voyage, well provided with the means of living in their new home, and, withal, buoyed up with the idea of soon being safely established in the very citadel of the true church. These infatuated people little dreamed their troubles were just commencing. The Mormon agent in St. Louis took a fancy to a very fine piano which Mrs. G. had, and induced her to leave it with him, under the pretense that the dry heat of the weather on the plains would ruin it. Of course, they have seen the last of it, or of its value.

They started on the plains, with a number of wagons loaded with their goods, drawn by cattle. But Mr. G. had none of the qualities of a good teamster—his hired men were brutal, and his animals gave out, one after the other, leaving their carcasses to the surgery of the wolves. His goods fell a prey to the rapacity of his companions, under one pretense and another, until they reached Bridger's, about one hundred miles from the promised land, nearly in a state of destitution. The mother's heart was full of foreboding: their comfortable future had withered away in a few short months, like the green leaf before the hot breath of a sirocco; and, to cap the climax, she had just learned that polygamy was a cherished institution in the church. To turn back, however, was impossible. Poor woman! she is destined, I fear, to be cured of her infatuated credulity by much deep suffering.

It is customary with Brigham, at the approach of an emigrating party, to go out a day's journey to meet them, with a band of music and fresh provisions. It enables him to make a show, and gives an air of triumph on the acquisition of numbers to his colony. So, in this instance, he went out, and met them, struggling through the mountain passes, with provisions and some delicious melons; and ushered them into the city, under a bright September sun, with music playing and banners flying. Their hearts were gladdened— there seemed to be a shout, as well as a smile, of welcome from the valley—but it was as the last flashing up of the lamp, before the flame of hope becomes utterly extinct.

A few days found them established in the smallest kind of an adobe house, wholly destitute of the appearance of comfort on the outside, and none within except what belonged to their neat and tidy habits. Mr. G. is one of the few we are always pleased to see; he

calls occasionally, and cannot conceal his
abhorrence of polygamy from ordinary pene-
tration. He is now struggling to eke out a
living—his days are spent copying the laws,
and his nights as an actor at the theatre—a
pandemonium more vile than the most prurient
imagination can conceive; but if he comes out
unscathed it will be a miracle. In a few
years, unless they make their escape, their
daughters will, one after the other, be distributed among the priesthood. If I could
make myself a Caligula, and hold the sword
of the executioner over these detestable villains, having but one neck for the convenience
of a single blow, I should be sorely tempted
just now to undergo the transformation.

LETTER XI.

GREAT SALT LAKE CITY, Feb., 1853.

I HAVE just heard a story of that wonderful saint, Parley Pratt, which, told anywhere else, or of anybody else, I would not credit for a moment. Here, however, where the ordinary rules of religion and morality are reversed—where roguery is commendable, and prostitution a virtue—I am justified in believing anything.

Some two years and a half ago, the redoubtable Parley was appointed to a mission in Chili; and though, on such occasions, they pretend to go without purse or scrip, as commanded in apostolic times, yet these are only pretenses for the uninitiated, and a pretext for the universal beggary which they practice. It happened in this emergency, that Parley's money market was in a crisis; but this was not the worst of it; he had borrowed so often, forgetting to pay, that his exceedingly bland manner had lost its influence. He was in a fair way of starting on his mission in a far more apostolic fashion than suited his inclinations.

But Parley is a man of resources under difficulties. His house was somewhat over-stocked with wives, and as they are a species of property here, having a marketable value, it occurred to him that he might drive a good bargain with Walker, the Indian chief, who, with a band of Utes, was holding a talk with the authorities of the city. He accordingly proposed to the chief to "*swap*" one of his white squaws for ten horses, a proposition which was at once accepted.

Martha, a good-natured English girl, was the inmate of his harem chosen for this exchange, and the heartless wretch informed her of the transaction, and bade her prepare for this new phase in her eventful life, with the smiling aspect with which he would have invited her to visit their next-door neighbor. The poor thing was greatly shocked. She had lived long enough with the brute to learn that he concealed, under a friendly garb, a heart of supreme indifference to the feelings and happiness of others; yet, to be spared such a fate, she prostrated herself before him in agonizing entreaty, though in vain.

A few days, however, intervened before the "swap" could be finally consummated, and these few days did the work of years upon the poor crushed woman. Her cheeks became sunken and pallid; her countenance exhibited the deep-drawn lines of unmistakable agony; and, finally, when she was brought face to face with Walker, with eyes red and swollen with weeping, the savage turned his back with disgust, saying, "*me no want old white squaw.*" The bargain fell through, and there is enough of secrecy hanging over the affair to enable the rascal, liar as he is, to deny that it ever had existence.

This notable expedient having failed, Parley was again in trouble; but just then he heard of a female friend, who had lately received a sum of money from some source, and from her he procured the requisite supplies, and proceeded to his post. His mission, however, proved unsuccessful. The Chilians turned a deaf ear, alike to the merits of Joseph Smith and the eloquence of the great Parley. His means finally melted away, and, in wandering back, he found himself at San Bernardino, in a state of great destitution. While waiting at this point a train came in from Salt Lake; and the wagon-master, who had gathered a few hundred dollars of hard earnings, was wheedled to place them in the itching palm of the wily hypocrite. With this timely supply, the baffled missionary purchased mules, and returned to his harem, the forgiving Martha ready and willing to draw the veil over her past trials. It is needless to say that the wagon-master has made unavailing efforts to obtain a repayment of his money.

A few evenings ago we were invited by Mrs. Snow to spend an evening with them, at Parley's house, and hear him read from a manuscript work on theology, which he was preparing for the press. This was too good an opportunity, to look into a Mormon harem, to be neglected. We were ushered into a large room, received by him with much suavity of manner, and introduced to five Mrs. Pratts in succession; one of whom assumed the office of mistress of ceremonies, taking our shawls, and inviting us to seats near the fire. The rest remained demurely seated after the ceremony of introduction, busily plied their knitting, and were as whist as mice while the cat is foraging for supplies. The mistress of the house was a Boston divorcée, who had left her husband and home for conscience' sake. Three of the bevy I judged to be English, and one was a fair-looking American girl. What a spectacle, and that, too, in our own country!

Parley seated himself at a candle-stand, in the centre of the room, and entertained us for some time with conversation in regard to the Chilians; some incidents of his journey; the peculiarities of the Spanish language, and so forth. He gave us a graphic description of a pass in the Sierra Nevada. The man has a very even flow of language, and converses with great ease. He read from his manuscript for nearly or quite half an hour, and certainly until I got heartily tired of it. The style was much like his conversation; but the matter was devoid of vitality, consisting of the most

8

external and lifeless misapplication of scripture texts to the support of his peculiar notions. If mankind were bodies of flesh, without souls, and like the beasts that perish, the Mormon scheme would be as well adapted to their government as any other.

I must not forget a notable incident of this notable interview. As we got up to go, and partly to busy myself about something while the ceremony of leave-taking was going on, I turned to the wall to look at a garish-looking daub, intended to represent human beings. Parley immediately came up with the light, and said it was a family group, and proceeded to point out that such a figure was such a mother, then present in the room, with her brood around her, and thus going through with the whole collection. His own burly figure was in the midst, and could be distinguished without the aid of the Dutchman's expedient. We were compelled, of course, to give the same degree of polite attention that would have been expected by a farmer at the East, in exhibiting a favorite flock of Shanghais, or litter of pigs.

On returning, Mrs. S., who is so far fortunate that, as yet, she is the sole wife in the family, and her sister, who was also of the party, were anxious that I should view Parley's females in the same light as married women in the States. I asked Mrs. S. if she, as a wife and mother, was willing that her own home should become the receptacle of such inmates, simply because they were called wives? Leaving her to reflect upon this question, which she was not prepared to answer, we soon bade good evening to our friends and threaded our way to our home.

The city was hushed into the stillness of repose; its mud-colored huts, and its spreading plain, and the towering hights, were silvered over with the soft light of the moon; and as we stood in our porch, and gazed upon the "Twin Peaks," glittering like huge diamonds in the sky, our thoughts rose far, far above the gross and filthy sphere of sensuality with which we had been surrounded.

10th. In the curious gathering from the four winds, which forms the population of this sequestered region, not the least interesting are a few families from Denmark. Any one, visiting a menagerie, naturally desires to get the worth of his money, and see all that is dear-bought and far-fetched. Yesterday I visited a Danish family, and partly from them, and partly from others, I have learned enough of their history to feel a strong sympathy for them. Of course they are victims of the numberless impositions practiced by the Mormon missionaries to induce credulous people to take up their abode in this den of iniquity.

Erastus Snow, a brother of Judge Snow, is the privateer who claims the honor of making this Danish prize. He is of the twelve, lives in one of the larger sized dwellings, having grounds tastefully arranged, and a few shade trees, which always attract our eyes in this treeless valley; has one wife in fact, and four women whom he calls wives; is a preacher of the genus Boanerges, ranting and roaring with great apparent zeal; and is as precious a scamp as any in the gang. He returned last fall from a successful foray in Norway and Denmark.

This Danish family, in their own country,

were in good circumstances, and above the common order in education and refinement; but, like many people in the north of Europe, had a great admiration for the institutions of this country, coupled with a growing discontent with those of their own, and were easily persuaded to emigrate. The wily missionary wormed himself completely into the confidence of the worthy Dane. He gave him a glowing account of the climate and fertility of the valley of the Great Salt Lake, of the flourishing condition of the Mormons, of the rigid purity of their morals, of the opportunity for building up a great fortune by investing his property in the church; but not a word about polygamy. He lived for months in his family, enjoyed his generous hospitality, drank his wines, and used his horses and his purse with all the freedom of long-established friendship. The simple Northman was no match for the unscrupulous cunning of the yankee follower of Joseph Smith. He made up his mind that the new religion was as good as any of the contradictory systems with which the world is perplexed, sold his estate, placed $10,000 in the hands of Elder Snow, to be invested in church property; collected together his household goods, and turned his back upon his native land, and his face towards the New World.

On going aboard the steamer, his family were turned with the common herd into the steerage, jostled to and fro in the general rush and scramble which belongs to such occasions. As soon as he could, he sought out, and found, the Mormon Elder upon deck, and accosted him somewhat angrily:

"You certainly could not have purchased steerage tickets for myself and family, with the money I gave you?"

"Surely not; you are merely put there temporarily till we sail, which will be this evening—the emigration fund will not allow any better accommodations for the rest of the saints, and they would grumble if we made any distinction."

This seemed plausible, and, with a bewildered air, he seated himself upon his luggage in the midst of his wife and children, whose *abandon* of grief, at parting from home and friends, made all parts of the vessel alike to them.

After the ship got under weigh, he went to the purser to get the number of their state-rooms. That important official looked over the list, and shook his head: "Sir, your name is not here."

"It must be there."

"No it is not. Whom did you purchase your ticket of?"

"I gave Elder Snow the money, with directions to procure two state-rooms."

"Well, all I can say is, you are in the steerage, and the Elder has the best state-room in the ship for himself—please to make room for others."

He made another effort to see the saintly Elder, but it was difficult crossing the absolute line of demarcation between cabin and steer-age, and he did not find him for some days. He was then told there was some mistake about it, which should be rectified, and in this way was put off from time to time, and finally lectured on the necessity of bear-ing patiently these minor inconveniences, in reference to the glorious consummation in prospect. Compelled to submit, they were landed in St. Louis, dissatisfied with their treatment; but they were utter strangers, and ignorant of the language, and were carried along in the stream of emigration to Salt Lake.

Here they are lodged in a wretched hut, which, they are assured, will be exchanged for a large and comfortable mansion in the ensuing summer. When I saw them yesterday, they looked the very picture of discomfort, and, I may add, despair. They were all huddled together, evidently unused to such extreme domestic emergencies. The table exhibited the remains of a scanty dinner; a splendid harp stood in the corner, with a sack of flour leaning against it for support, *vis-à-vis* with a valuable painting. They have made some disagreeable discoveries. They have discovered that the money which the husband placed in Snow's hands is the beginning of his tithing, and belongs to the church; that a house is to be built for him, if he wants it, for which he will be in debt to the church; that their daughter is approaching a marriageable age, and will soon be needed in Elder

Snow's harem; that their hands are in the lion's mouth, and will remain there for some time.

The mother pointed to a fair, sweet-looking, flaxen-haired girl of sixteen, and made me understand, in her broken English, that their neighbor, a great burly Briton, had made proposals to her to be his sixth wife, the five favored mortals already under his roof being, at the same time, in a state bordering on starvation. The young thing exhibited a look of disgust and terror at the prospect before her; but the crushing weight of persecution will be brought to bear upon them, and there is too much reason to fear that the poor girl is destined to a life of shame.

The Englishman alluded to is a very fair comic actor at their saturnalian theatre, and is, withal, a mechanic of more than ordinary ingenuity. It would be difficult to describe the huts in which his real and sealed wives are kept. On the boards, full of beef, beer, and fat, he acted the good-natured, rollicking Paddy to the life, and you would suppose his disposition all sunshine, and his life all charity

8*

to his race.   But, like the rest here, he is
fairly embarked upon the Styx, and as Charon
has charge of the boat, it is quite easy to
perceive his final landing-place.

This reminds me of another conspicuous
John Bull, who rejoices in the name of Bul-
lock, and is the private secretary of his Mormon majesty, the great Brigham.   He, too,
is sleek and well fed ; looks as if he lived
near the tithing office, where good things are
stored away for the benefit of the knowing
ones.   This man is short, round, dapper, and
bustling, reminding one of a fussy, noisy little
humble-bee, which proclaims to all the world
that he is engaged in the important business
of gathering honey.   This little man has some
rhetorical pretensions, which smack of cock-
neyism, and makes quite an oration when he
calls at our quarters on business.   He puts
me in mind of Sir Geoffrey Hudson, immor-
talized by Scott, who, though small in stature,
was ambitious of great things.   The saints
think he has something in him worth cherish-
ing.   At the party at Social Hall, his wife
had such an unhappy look, mingled with an

assumed appearance of gayety, while he was
dancing with a second he had lately taken in,
that it attracted my attention. Her plumes
and gay pink head-dress fairly trembled like
the aspen, with suppressed agitation—I expected every moment to hear her shriek wildly
and despairingly in the violence of her emotions.

Feb. 21st. Yesterday morning we were invited by our acquaintance, Colborn, to attend
the wedding of his daughter to a man by the
name of Pomeroy, who already has a wife.
The affair was to come off at two o'clock,
and we went, of course, with the expectation
of witnessing the ceremonies on such occasions; but in this we were cheated—it proved
to be the wedding feast, the marriage ceremony
having been performed in the forenoon. It
would be difficult to imagine a scene exhibiting deeper evidence of depravity, folly, and
wretchedness.

We had some difficulty in finding Colborn's
house. It was over a mile south from Mr.
Farnham's, and though the day was fair, yet
the ground was soft and spongy, and the

numerous water-courses had broken over their bounds, and, in some places, flooded the streets. On reaching the house, we were directed across the way, to the residence of Colborn's new son-in-law, where the company were to assemble, previous to the feast. Here we found Brigham Young, with his first wife, and some eight or ten other persons; and, among the rest, the creature whose gaze through the window troubled me so much, soon after our arrival in the city.

This was, without exception, the strangest party it was ever my fortune to attend, and the chief point of interest was the real wife of the man who had just been married to another. It is difficult to give you an idea of the emotions of this suffering woman. Her face was as white as chalk—her eyes were as black as jet, and glittered with an unearthly lustre. She tried to exhibit a cheerful expression, and had evidently nerved herself up, like the Indian at the stake, to endure the torture of her situation. The nervous twitching of the muscles of her mouth betrayed a degree of internal agony, which it was, to me, painful to contemplate. That face will, I fear, haunt me in my dreams—the intensity of her suffering had made it rigid. The cords of her life must soon snap asunder—the sooner the better. This wedding was evidently the funeral of all her hopes.

The husband is manifestly a shallow-pate, made up of animal and man, and the latter a small fraction. His new wife, poor, silly thing, cuddled down by him, and he manifested a boorish pleasure, mingled with that kind of shamefacedness common, I suppose, to henroost thieves. But Brigham was there to keep him in countenance in the profane presence of us two Gentiles, who had a difficult task to suppress the scorn and contempt which we felt.

How shall I describe Mrs. Young? She was richly though not fashionably or tastefully dressed, and wrapped herself up in a cold reserve, conversing in monosyllables, which came out painfully under the merciless cross-examination in which I felt at liberty to indulge. But "yes" and "no" furnish but small data to judge of human char-

acter, and about all I can say of her is, that
she is rather large in size, and good-looking
for her age. The woman, evidently, has little
refinement, but she does not lack sense, and
felt oppressed with the idea that we despised
the whole concern. Brigham had his share of
the same degree of constraint; but he put on a
"you can't help yourself" sort of bearing, and
conversed with some degree of fluency.

Colborn, who is a species of dotard harlequin, was anxious that the occasion should
be a joyous one, and skipped about like an
overgrown ourang-outang, making all sorts of
nonsensical observations, some of which, I
could see, Brigham did not like at all. He
tried hard to get up a dance; and, although
there was a fiddler present, every one's heels
seemed to be glued to the floor. He alleged,
however, that it would not do to have a wedding without dancing; so he set the fiddle to
sawing, and danced a jig himself, all alone.
What a pitiable spectacle of degradation and
shame! Here was the head-impostor and
bashaw of fifty wives and upwards—here was
a poor wife suffering agonies too great to be

endured—and here was a father, dancing a merry jig over the prostitution of his own daughter; and all this, too, in a city constituting a part and portion of our beloved country.

The dinner came off at the house of this delectable father-in-law, at the time appointed, and was good enough. Not to be laid under obligation by such people, my husband paid him what he supposed a fair compensation for the entertainment, which was greedily accepted; and we had the good fortune to get back to our comfortable quarters before night, fully satisfied with our further initiation into the mysteries of Mormonism.

LETTER XII.

GREAT SALT LAKE CITY, March 1, 1853.

To-DAY we have been walking out in the warm sunshine; the air is bland; Mrs. Farnham and Father Lee are gardening, and you are shivering under one of those cold northwestern blasts, the bare remembrance of which is enough to freeze one's blood.

I find a marked difference between our hostess and the Mormon women here. She is energetic, and careful for the comfort of her family. Yesterday I had a long walk with her, and among other places we went to Sayres' garden with a Mrs. Van C., who keeps a boarding-house for Gentiles (her husband being on a mission), and is reputed neat and thrifty. But she spoke with so much languor and despondency, that I suspected the skeleton, which some one speaks of as being in every house, had manifested its ghostly presence in her own. She complained bitterly of poverty; and expressed anxiety in reference to being able to provide her children with bread.

"What is the use," said she, "of slaving myself; Van C., like all the rest, will bring home a number of spirituals. I am surprised, sister Farnham, you can keep up such a flow of spirits, for I suppose your husband has left you to provide for yourself for the next five years."

"Certainly he has, and I get along quite as well—if I can't live here, I will go to my sister in California."

This Mrs. Van C. is lady-like in her manners, but fragile in form, and poorly calculated to battle for bread in such a place as this. It slipped out, during the conversation, that some of the dignitaries had intimated, that women, whose husbands were long absent, had duties to perform peculiar to Mormon institutions: and that, if she was more complying in this respect, her pathway would be rendered smooth. What an abyss of abomination!

Sayres, in whose pleasant garden we were sauntering, is as much out of place as a jewel in a swine's snout. He perfectly detests the saints, all and sundry, and only came here because his wife became a convert to their absurd notions, and would be content nowhere else. Gardening is his ruling passion; he is an extravagant lover of flowers; finds many a floral *rara avis* in this region, and is making an extensive collection of plants, peculiar to the Great Basin, that will be valuable to botanists. It was a treat to see his forcing beds, and his fine display of vegetables just starting up, and arranged with that degree of neatness and taste peculiar to the ardent horticulturist. While I was expressing pleasure at the sight, he said in the States it would pay, but in a community of leeches, whose eternal cry was Give, Give, and no thanks, it was a hard business.

I tried to get an inkling of his wife's motives for coming here from her own lips, but she manifested so much unwillingness to say anything to me, that I gave it up. From Aunty Shearer, I learn that Mrs. S. was a Bostonian of Yankee shrewdness in some things, connected with many unprofitable idiosyncrasies; in common parlance, her mental machi-

nery had a great many "screws loose;" and
that is the case with the most of them. Like
the mass of emigrants, they entered the valley
poor. Soon after their arrival, Mrs. S. received, from some eastern resource, a sum of
money sufficient to have made them very comfortable. They built an adobe house, with a
small portion of it, and all the rest the foolish
woman loaned to Parley Pratt, whose powers
of suction, where money is concerned, are equal
to the most active of the blood-sucker kind;
he is like a sponge, with one important difference—in having great capacity for absorption,
without allowing anything to be squeezed out
of him.

I am tired and weary of gathering up incidents of personal history in this place—it is
all alike—it is just one unvarying picture of
rascality, folly, imposition, credulity and crime.
And you, too, must be equally tired in reading
the sketches which I give you. I will try to
get rid of this monotony, though the chances
are that I shall find myself gliding back into
it, as easily as a carriage slides back into an
ugly rut which disfigures the road.

March 5th.   We are just now in high spirits.
Our friend, Mr. Livingston, has decided to start
on the first of May with a train of cattle for
California, and we are to go with him.   There
will be from sixty to one hundred men; more
than enough, at any rate, for safety, and it
is said we shall reach San Francisco early in
July.   The prospect of escaping from this region of moral pestilence, at a period much
earlier than we anticipated, has almost lifted
me into the clouds.   In addition, we have,
within a few days, formed the acquaintance
of a Mr. and Mrs. McP., who are Gentiles—
temporary sojourners—he engaged in all kinds
of trading, and she lively, intelligent, and having about the same opinion of the saints that
we entertain.

The spring opens with great beauty: everything blooms in the valley, while the sur-
rounding mountains are robed in white.   The
snow has been receding on these lofty heights
for some time.   The mountains here furnish
a scale by which the progress of spring and
summer can be measured.   The snow-line
gradually retreats to the top; but they say

the "Twin Peaks," which majestically tower above the neighboring elevations, retain their snowy crown during the whole year.

In looking from our north window on the plateau, it is one glow of a delicate pink color, with scarce a tinge of green. On walking up there this morning, we found this ruddy carpet to consist of myriads of the tiniest flowers, opening their buds thus early. In this thicket of bloom, the sego plant shoots up its needle-like stem here and there, and in spots we find the expanding leaves of plants that are strange to us.

This plateau stretches along the base of the mountains, south, as far as the eye can reach, and was evidently once the shore of the lake, then, of course, a great inland sea. The region is so manifestly volcanic that the geologist can find but few of the remains of organic life. We picked up a very good specimen of coralline, belonging to the olden time, showing a delicate and fan-like tracery, from a common centre. These little insects must have been as much noted for industry, in the misty ages of a far-off antiquity, as at pre-

sent. How wonderfully is the evidence of
their instinctive skill imbedded in stone, more
enduring than the monuments of human cele-
brities !

In our stroll, we came to an emigrant wagon
just in from the valley of the Weber, where,
in one of the lateral gorges of the mountain,
the family have spent a lonely winter.   They
were from the pleasant banks of the Ohio,
the preceding summer; got snowed up forty
miles from here in October; have had a pre-
carious living on fish and game; and have
now just wallowed through the snow-obstruct-
ed cañon in search of food.   It was a traveling
household, with the usual collection of traps,
and the mistress of the migrating tenement
was at home. I said to her:

"You are not going to remain long here,
are you?"

"Well, I don't know as it'll make much difference—we're pretty comfortable; my man's
out herdin' cattle, and son's lookin' up work,
and as for me, I've got all my work done up
and am goin' to take a nap."

I queried again—"Where is your sewing or

knitting? How can you content yourself without doing something?"

She yawned and said: "You are a Gentile, ain't you? Why labor for the meat that perisheth? We are sojourners, for a season. The lilies toil not, neither do they spin," etc.

Thus ended the colloquy with this interesting specimen of womanhood, and thus has ended many a similar one in which I have taken part. Such women form a goodly portion of the mortar with which the bricks of the Mormon temple are cemented together. They are the contented portion of the harem, and must, I fancy, claim maternity to a very stupid or vicious race of descendants.

March 20. To-day we have had a long walk up City Creek, my husband with his fishing rod, and I with my curiosity, the weather being about equal to our first of May at home. The stream is rapid and beautiful, and runs from a wild gorge on the north side of the city, into which we passed, along the banks of the principal canal, conducting the water for distribution into our part of the town. At the end of the canal we found a road, leading to some wood a long way up the cañon. The creek was full of trout, but they seemed to have no appetite for Gentile bait, and we threaded our way leisurely along the road, which wound around very irregularly among a perfect labyrinth of hillocks, rising one above another interminably. We reached an elevation sufficient to find patches of snow, which appeared in still greater quantities further up.

In our stroll, we encountered an Indian, hunting; and I was childish enough to feel timid, as we were at least a mile and a half from the mouth of the cañon, and out of all sight or hearing of the city. He proved to be a young, well-formed, and not bad looking Ute, and readily enough, and with apparent good humor, entered into such conversation as we could hold, with a few words and many signs. I took out a pencil and paper, and gave him to understand that I wanted to sketch him, and it was curious to see into what a graceful attitude he placed himself, leaning on his rifle, and how pleased he was with the very rude production of my impromptu effort.

These Utes we meet with almost every day. They are wretched-looking objects, often squatting down in the very middle of the streets, devouring their food like dogs. All human beings, I believe, have a spark of pride, however low and degraded they may seem. I said to one yesterday, " You are a ' *Digger*.' " He raised himself with offended dignity, and said, " *Shoshonic—Shoshonie.*" "Digger" is a term as offensive to them as " nigger" to our poor Africans. Their papooses, with eyes glittering like little snakes, have humanity about them, for I can make them smile, like other babies, by chirping to them. The poor things are great beggars, and as a general rule the inhabitants are very charitable towards them.

In these walks there is an oppressive loneliness, on account of the absence of trees and birds. Very few of the feathered race are to be seen, except the everlasting crow, which croaks over and around us at every turn, as if depredation and prey were the ruling characteristics of the region. In our ramble to-day, we were delighted to hear the clear whistle of the meadow lark. and the occasional trill

9

and twitter of two or three other summer birds. Our landlady tells us the robin will soon make its appearance.

It has been said that birds, on account of their keenness of vision, ease and rapidity of motion, and elevation as it were, above the earth, correspond to the intellectual principle in the mind. This nearly universal absence of the feathered tribe, except those of the scavenger kind, may well typify the Mormon intellect, steeped as it is in sensuality. But, perhaps I am seeking a fanciful cause for what may be easily accounted for in the want of trees. Paradise itself must have been birdless, had it been treeless. Who would live where there are no forests? These eternal savannas, though surrounded by grand ranges of snow-mantled mountains, become dreadfully wearisome.

April 2. Yesterday we went to Salt Lake. This may sound paradoxical, inasmuch as, in common parlance, we have spent the winter "at Salt Lake," yet, until now, we have been no nearer that celebrated body of water than twenty-two miles. The expedition was planned by Mrs. McP. and myself; we literally "joined teams." Two of our mules were harnessed with two of theirs, into their carriage, and with a bountiful supply for a picnic upon the lake shore, we crossed the Jordan bridge near the city at an early hour, and rolled smoothly over the plain. This plain, however, was found to have its inequalities—there were an inconvenient number of small miry depressions, strongly impregnated with saleratus, which plagued us not a little, and two or three large ponds, filled with countless fowl, which rose up in clouds as we rode along, filling the air with their screams. It must be a perfect paradise for the sportsman.

We took the road which leads to Antelope Island. The island reared its mountain form before us, and after we had traveled for hours seemed no nearer. Gradually, however, its outlines became more boldly relieved against the sky, and the rocks, ravines, and inequalities upon its sides began to assume distinctness and shape, like the landscape, from which the misty twilight of early morning is fast receding. The lake, too, began to stretch away to the northwest, as far as the eye could reach; and, after wading laboriously through some miles of deep sand, we found ourselves upon its shores.

A strong south wind had swept the waters to the north, leaving a broad space of the bottom perfectly bare; this was crusted over with salt, which sparkled in the sun like innumerable diamonds. Our driver found the fording place to the island and plunged in, and on we went until it seemed to me the waters were too deep for safety. We halted to debate the question of a further prosecution of the journey. We were really *in* the Great Salt Lake, over which had hung such a cloud of mystery, and about which so many marvels had been related by early *voyageurs*, of terrible whirlpools and submarine grumblings. To us it was a very harmless sort of a water monster. A picnic on Antelope Island would be a very pretty thing to talk about at home; but to get swamped in trying to get there would end all stories on the subject. Prudence prevailed—we filled a bottle from the " briny deep," took a homœopathic taste all around, and then wheeled about. The mules, and carriage, and whatever else received a splash of the water, were coated white with salt.

Back again upon the shore, we found a place covered with sage bushes—picketed our animals, built a fire, made a strong dish of tea, and, in addition to sharp appetites, seasoned our dinner with free and easy remarks about the saints, entirely unapprehensive of espionage. Where, you will say, did you get the water to make your tea? A shrewd question. We brought with us a number of cans of the precious liquid, and had enough to give our patient mules a few swallows to wash down their scanty dinner. We are old campaigners, and all this was done up with the least possible waste of time, and, after gathering a few early wild flowers, we rolled back again to " Zion in the tops of the mountains."

The view to the north was uninterrupted to a great distance, and the mountains, stretching away south, lay "voluminous and vast," their snowy tops glittering in the rays of the sun. There they repose in stern and gloomy grandeur, the store-house of storms, and of the thousand streams that dash and hurry down upon the thirsty plains.

At the south we had a fine view of the rounded and heaped up masses, like thunder clouds, which bound the Utah lake. Nature has laid herself out here upon a great scale. In outline there is nothing little—everything is massive, mighty, grand.

At the base of the mountains, directly in front, lay the city, just discernible, melted together into a confused mass. As we traveled toward it, the view to the north contracted. A little to the northeast a thin, white vapor, like the spray of a spouting whale upon the ocean, indicated the presence of the hot spring. Gradually it assumed more distinctness, and finally rolled up in a compact volume, like the vapor from a locomotive in the frosty air, and was whirled away by the brisk south wind. Silvery threads, too, started out from the mighty canvas before us, as the dashing and spray-like streams, from the banks of snow, became discernible. Then the prominent buildings in the city came into view, and separated themselves from the rest; little patches and shades of green, from the ornamental trees, made their appearance; finally the dwellings ranged themselves in regular rows, the streets opened to view, we rolled over Jordan bridge and found ourselves once more in the Mormon capital.

April 5. I did not intend to say another word about the saints, male or female, but I was tempted yesterday to attend a meeting of the Council of Health, and am so full of what I saw and heard, that it will be a relief to give a brief account of it. This Council of Health, as it is called, is a sort of female society, something like our Dorcas societies, whose members have meetings to talk over their occasional various aches and pains, and the mode of cure. There are a few who call themselves physicians in the place, and they are privileged to a seat in this important assemblage.

The meeting was in one of the ward schoolhouses. There were from forty to fifty present, old and young, and, judging from physiognomical indications, they all, with two or three exceptions, belonged to the lowest class of ignorance. There seemed to be no redeeming qualities. The elder were destitute of those mild, refined, and softened feelings which often form such an agreeable relief to old age. The specimens before me were of the wrinkled, spiteful, hag-like order—time had evidently laid a rough and relentless hand upon them. The younger portion were to me, if anything, more repulsive still—there was no youthful vivacity of appearance or manner. They were stupid, and sensuality had swallowed up all pure womanly feelings.

The meeting was called to order by Dr. Richards, a hoary-headed old sinner, whose looks were sufficiently sanctified to remind you of some of our good deacons at home—but you must not fancy a further resemblance. He made a strange opening for a Council of Health. He said they were in the midst of dangerous times—that trouble was brewing for the saints, by disaffected spirits, and, if they were not cut off before their plans ripened, the devil would reign again. At this interesting climax, he brought his hand down as though he intended, then and there, to punch a hole through the heads of one of these spirits. He managed to get up so much ferocity of expression, that I was relieved when he sat down.

A Dr. Sprague, a man having a look of vulgar dissipation, then rose and made a few common-place remarks about health. In the mean time, the women began to manifest much uneasiness, twisting, weaving, and rocking to and fro, as though they intended to do something effective when they got a chance. As soon as Dr. S. sat down, sister Newman bounded up like a cork, and, in spiteful and sharp tones, said that Mormon women ought not to be subject to pain, but that disease and death must be banished from among them, and go to the Gentiles, where they belonged; that God would soon glorify his name by cutting off the rotten nations of the earth; and then the women would obey their husbands, love them, wait on them, and, if they wanted more wives, help to get them. It was a rambling tirade, and there was enough more of the same kind—but I can only report the

9*

substance. She was succeeded by sister Susanna Lippincot, one of Dr. Richards's houris, and a fair specimen of the degraded class of spiritual wives. One of the sisters near me whispered, "She is full of the spirit." I could easily see that she was full of spirits that came from the distillery. She advocated pouring down lobelia until the devils were driven out of the body. She fastened her red, gooseberry eyes upon me, and made some ill-natured remarks about the Gentiles. She finally broke forth into an unknown tongue, and, as near as I can recollect, these were the words: "*Eli, ele, elo, ela—come, coma, como—reli, rele, rela, relo—sela, selo, sele, selum.*" This gibberish was repeated over two or three times.

Sister Sessions then arose and translated these mysterious words. The interpretation proved to be a mere repetition of what the inspired Susanna had before said in murdered English. Sister Sessions took her seat, and sister Gibbs got up, fully possessed, to overflowing, with the notion of healing, even to the mending of broken limbs, by faith and the laying on of hands. By some unlucky mishap, her arm had been dislocated, and she roundly asserted that it had been instantaneously put into its place by this divine process. But alas! exercise had put her arm out of joint a second time, and she piteously bemoaned her fate with tears, lest the Lord might not condescend to heal her again. She was a wretched case of crazy fanaticism. Others poured forth incoherent nonsense in the same strain.

One woman had a daughter present, who was badly afflicted with scrofula, and expressed a wish to have the remedy applied. The sisters crowded around, and, with the two brothers, laid their right hands upon her, and prayed very much like the Catholics repeating their Aves and Pater Nosters over their beads. Dr. Sprague was then moved by the spirit to bless the patient in an unknown tongue, pronouncing, in a blatant tone, words something like these: "*Vavi, vava, vavum—sere, seri, sera, serum.*" The same sister, who had already acted as interpreter, gave the meaning to these oracular utterances. They proved to be the invocation of great blessings, both temporal and spiritual; she was to have everything that heart could desire; her seed was to outnumber the hosts of Abraham, Isaac, and Jacob. Poor thing, she looked as though she needed some better guaranty for temporal comforts than these empty sounds. She could not have been over eighteen; had a large baby in her lap and another child at home; was poorly clad, and undoubtedly half fed.

My guide-book, Aunty Shearer, was with me. She, too, made some remarks, which, to do her justice, were a good deal more to the purpose. Sister Sessions again took the floor, and related a dream of the night before, of a remarkable fight between the Lord and the devil. His sooty majesty came pretty near obtaining the mastery, but was finally overcome, and, as the moral of the affair, the Lord advised her to use lobelia in curing disease, as that would drive the devil away. With this crowning dose the meeting adjourned.

This is a faithful account of the meeting, except that I have been compelled to soften down some of the expressions used, which were too gross to be repeated. It has given me the horrors. I begin to have a superstitious dread that we may be in some way prevented from leaving at the time appointed, and our stay in this place indefinitely prolonged.

April 30. To-morrow we turn our backs upon the Mormon capital, with its wretchedness, abominations, and crimes. We have formed a few friendly acquaintances, with whom we part with regret; but oh! how rejoiced to escape from a region of human depravity, the terrible features of which have opened more and more distinctly to view the longer our sojourn has continued.

Our arrangements are all made. To-morrow we resume our wandering life, in the same traveling mansion which brought us here, drawn by the same patient mules, under the superintendence of the same faithful Morse; and for the next six or eight weeks we must thread our way through the Great Basin. What the future has in store we know not, but our hearts are light, and our trust is in Providence.

LETTER XIII.

SALT LAKE CITY TO BEAR RIVER.

BEAR RIVER, May 10, 1853.

WE have traveled from Great Salt Lake City to Bear River in almost an extacy of delight. No holiday pleasure excursion can begin to compare with it. Before leaving the Mormon capital, I had become quite childish in regard to our prospects of getting away—I was really superstitious, and observant of signs and omens, fancying that something would turn up, to prevent our egress from this mountain-girt region. This feeling increased in intensity, as the time for departure arrived; and it seems to me now, I must have gone into a regular fit of hysterics, had the event been delayed for a single day. You must recollect the time had already been postponed.

The first arrangement was for the train to

start as early as the 25th of April, and, with
this view, Mr. Livingston had sent his wagon-
master, Capt. Egan, and one of his clerks, Ed-
gar Blodget, early in the month, to Bridger's,
to procure a quantity of cattle for his drove.
After they had been absent longer than seemed
necessary, vague rumors of disaster began to
float in, nobody knew how, and Mr. L. in
alarm started off to look after their safety.
He had a dismal time of it, and found his
agents at the fort; but they had suffered
dreadfully. They became involved in the
deep snow, lost their way, exhausted their
provisions, and were actually ten days in
sight of the fort in a state of starvation.
They crawled for miles on their hands and
knees, and finally came in with lacerated
bodies and badly frozen feet — Egan's so
badly that he is unable to walk a step without the aid of crutches. About the same time,
a party of Mexicans came in from the Rio
Colorado, in not much better condition, and
reported several of their companions frozen
to death some twenty miles from the fort.
Mr. L. says we can form no conception of

the immense masses of snow which have accumulated in the mountains.

These misadventures occasioned the delay, and it was quite easy for me to fancy others equally formidable. To cap the climax, Mr. F. had a chill about nine o'clock of the newly-appointed day, and we were to start at two—an ominous drawback—but he took a cold water pack—an application which had before proved efficacious—and was resolute to go.

For days previous Morse exercised the mules, to bring them back again to proper discipline, and get through with the preliminary mishaps to harness, and other needful etcetera, which are apt to occur at the commencement of such an expedition; and we made two or three little excursions in the environs of the city. Once we went to the hot spring, about three miles on the California road. It smoked in the distance like a steamboat. Should the boiler below explode some day, they will have a choice earthquake or two, to register among the phenomena of the valley. Perhaps a volcano will rear its conical head, and shoot forth its lurid artillery to the sky. It pours out a large volume of water, from beneath a shelving mass of soft rock, formed of limy and salt accretions from the water, and is unbearably hot. A small lake formed from it, on the lower side of the road, swarmed with water fowl, which screamed all sorts of discordances.

When we got all ready to start, Mrs. Snow and Aunty Shearer came in to bid us goodby. Mrs. S. was anxious to obtain from me a expression on a particular point: she asked me if I could not be induced to believe that the spirituals, who are sincere in the belief of Mormonism, are without blame, and, therefore, to be regarded as *wives*, because they supposed themselves to be so. It was no time for a collision on any subject; so I said that ignorance might furnish some excuse, but that the men who were keeping up the delusion deserved the severest punishment. This did not mend the matter much, because it assumed that the whole thing was an imposture. Aunty Shearer squared herself for a regular battle for the faith; but Mr. F. interposed, assuring them we had full confidence in the sincerity of those present; but they must consider we were

Gentiles, and looked upon it from a very different point of view, and must, therefore, excuse us.

We parted with Mrs. Farnham with emotion on both sides. She has treated us with sisterly kindness throughout: I cannot now recall any want of attention to our least wants. We shall never see her again—nor shall we ever forget her. The children, too, hang around us, and excited more regret at leaving than we supposed possible.

The train started two days in advance of us. Its movements, at first, were slow, because it requires a short period to bring such a body of men and animals into a state of organization and discipline. Sundry things, too, are generally overlooked, and have to be sent back for. The banks of the Weber were appointed as the final rendezvous, where all the scattered components of our cavalcade were to be gathered, and from that point go on in conjunction. Mr. L. staid behind a week to await the arrival of the mail, which was looked for daily when we left.

Capt. Egan, the conductor of our train, may

fairly be termed a mountaineer. He has been back and forth from Missouri to Salt Lake, and from the latter to California, with the mail and with cattle, sundry times; and is reputed to be among the most experienced and safe for such an enterprise. The crippled condition of his feet compels him to ride in a wagon— a few times he has mounted a horse, but complains of great pain. He is a Mormon; but we have a hint that his Mormonism sits sufficiently light upon him to see that we poor Gentiles are properly cared for. So far he has been exceedingly attentive to our slightest wants. His wife accompanied us a few stages, and assisted Dr. Coward in dressing his feet.

This Dr. Coward is an under-sized Englishman, who makes great pretensions to skill, and bustles about largely, both morning and evening, in attending upon his patients. His face is suspiciously ruddy, and his nose richly carbuncled, indicating deep internal potations. How he got to Salt Lake, I do not know; but have learned that he has a brother there who, having a wife in England, has taken

another among the saints. The Doctor de-
nounces Mormonism, the country, and all that
is in it, and thinks his brother is in a dreadful
fix. What have been the nature of his own
predicaments in his native country, and since
he left it, I shall, of course, not trouble my
head about; but I may be pardoned, under
the circumstances, if I look even to this low
specimen of John Bullism, for some of the
amusements of the long journey before us.
I see he is not to be one of our mess in the
camp, and in this, as in a hundred other
things, we can trace the minute arrangements
which Mr. L. has made for our comfort.

Another companion of the journey is Dr.
H——, who belongs to our mess, and in whom
we feel more than ordinary interest. He was
once a Mormon, or at least tried to think he
was, and is now taking final leave of that
hopeful fraternity. He is a first-rate dentist,
is a man of some education, abounds in good
feelings, and is lively and witty in conversation. In the States he met with adverse
fortune, and, after being buffeted about roughly for a time, he found himself among the

Latter Day Saints, as a species of last and desperate resort; and, being of a skeptical inclination of mind, he joined them because he concluded their religion to be as good as any afloat. It seemed to be a fair point for the practice of his profession, so he bought a house and lot, and thought himself in a fair way of being snugly settled for life. But the rough points of his new brotherhood eventually became as unbearable as the barrel of spikes to which poor Regulus was treated by the Carthaginians. He found a respectable amount of business, but no pay; and was cheated in all imaginable ways. He became acquainted and was brought into contact with every conceivable kind of rascality; and, becoming utterly disgusted with his new associates, he made up his mind to leave them.

During the winter he came often to our quarters, and aided us in passing the time pleasantly. As the period for departure approached, the Doctor became almost womanishly nervous, lest the rascals should prevent his departure, by cutting his harness, poisoning his mules, instituting sham legal proceedings, or in some other way embarrass his movements; and he has so often repeated that, if he was only *over Bear River*, he would feel safe, that "over Bear River" became with us a phrase as significant as "over Jordan." This river, though not the geographical boundary of Brigham's pontificate, is practically regarded as the limit of his sway in this direction.

We have also a specimen of womankind, as Monkbarns would say, in the person of Mrs. Kinney, who came from England to make salvation secure by gathering with the saints. She acts in the capacity of cook to our mess. All I shall ask of her is civility and neatness, and as yet she seems duly qualified in both respects. Her husband is along as "master of the horse," and, as we have some noble specimens in the train, his time is fully taken up with his charge.

We started on the 5th, with that kind of exhilaration usually felt at the commencement of a pleasant trip. The day was superbly fine, not a cloud to be seen, and the mountains flashing their snowy tops in the sunlight. We passed around the elbow of the mountain

range, on the lower step of which the city
is built, and went directly north — bidding
adieu, in passing, first to the warm springs,
which had furnished the luxury of a bath, and
then to the hot springs, whose ever-ascending
vapor is such a remarkable addition to the
scenery. Morse was in high feather, flourishing his long whip; and the mules dashed
along as though they, too, felt elated in
escaping from the Mormon dominions. We
passed for some fifteen miles at the base of
the mountain, and then diverged to the left
towards the lake, to the residence of a Mr.
Hayt, of whom we had engaged some choice
butter for our own use, and where we spent
the night. This man is a large farmer, living
in a fair-sized adobe house within a mile of the
lake. A very pretty stream coursed rapidly
a few rods in the rear; and, as it was lined
with a small growth of trees, the whole scene
looked more like eastern life than we usually
see. On the other side of the way was a
large and convenient barn, and the yard adjacent contained some fine Durham and Devon
cows; and we are told that the Mormon settle-

ments are well provided with imported breeds
of cattle.

We were hospitably entertained, and pressingly invited to sleep within the walls of the building; but our traveling bed-room was ready for
use, and we thought it as well to make a
beginning there as at the end of the next
stage.   The family is rigidly Mormon, but
there is but one wife; and I was told, before
leaving the city, that she was an eastern
woman, and would return to the States on
a visit to her friends, but for the apprehension
of his taking another in her absence.   She was
manifestly sore on this subject; and I fancied
the servant girl looked and acted as though
she was a candidate for promotion.   Mrs. H.,
however, is evidently a tartar; and if there
is not warm work when the kitchen-maid
gains the right of *entré* to the parlor, I shall
think some change has taken place in human
nature.

This is the last house we shall probably
enter before reaching California.   We left it
the next morning, on a good road along the
lake—the ascending vapor of the hot spring

hanging like a thin veil of gauze at the base
of the mountains, and the city just dimly
visible in the rear. After traveling about
ten miles, we were overtaken by Dr. H.,
who staid behind to complete his arrangements, and together we continued the route
in pursuit of the train. Winding our way
along to the right, towards the mountains,
some five miles, we finally descended into
the valley of the Weber, near the immense
gorge from which it issues forth, and found
the train on the banks of the stream, in one
of the loveliest spots imaginable. There were
a goodly number of acres perfectly level, richly
carpeted with grass, upon which the cattle
were feeding with great apparent satisfaction;
in front a handsome belt of trees lined the
river up and down; and, to the right, at a
short distance, arose the mountains, buttressed
with frowning rocks, and the summits covered
with snow.

We reached the camp early enough to have
two or three little strolls in search of wild
flowers and odd looking pebbles, along the
margin of the stream. The banks are exceed-

10

ingly steep and precipitous, and the water courses along with the rapidity of a raceway. Our men had great difficulty in forcing the mules down to the water to drink. Mrs. Kinney busied herself in arranging her housekeeping appointments, which proved to be ample in amount and quality. She superintends a huge wagon, which we all call "the kitchen," and in which are stored away the furniture for the table, with a multitude of eatables. She found matters very much at heads and points, and said it would take two or three days to get everything into regular order. The immense vehicle, drawn by any number of oxen, furnishes her, also, with a sleeping apartment. Our supper, about sunset, was served on a camp table—a very convenient affair, which is taken to pieces and put together again with great ease—around which we were comfortably seated in chairs.

Soon after, the men gathered the cattle into an immense "corral," which some herder had erected in this beautiful pasture ground, consisting of upright logs, stockade fashion. Darkness thickened around us; and, disturbed only by the lowing of the herd, we quietly passed the first night with the train.

The next morning we crossed the Weber on a bridge, and then we had a rough and troublesome causeway of brush and poles for half a mile, through a wet piece of ground. This place had been talked about before we started, as very dangerous in miring animals, and, of course, was a subject of dread; but it had been rendered more safe by the falling of the river and some repairs. These difficulties over, we had a pleasant road for the rest of the day.

The Ogden river, a much smaller stream, we forded with ease; and passed Ogden city —a merely thickly-settled neighborhood, but which flourishes largely upon paper, among Mormon cities. Our day's travel was near the mountains—huge battlements, raising their crests to the sky—their sides seamed with wavy thread lines, made by the moccasined feet of the Indians in finding their way to their inaccessible dens and *wick-ee-ups*,* reminding you of the stealthy panther seeking his lair.

* Wigwams.

Among the noted places of the region is Ogden's Hole—a quiet, sequestered nook of the cañon from which the river flows; and celebrated for one or more of those desperate encounters between mountaineers and savages which are fast becoming traditionary. It is noted, too, for one of those rough romances which belong to savage and half civilized life of more recent date. The story goes, that one of the roving white hunters, some five or six years ago, became attached to and married the daughter of a chief, and lived in this retreat, with much apparent contentment. He acquired great influence over the natives; joined them in their hunts and sports; contended successfully with the grisly bear; brought down the mountain sheep from the highest crag; and drew the largest and brightest trout from the stream. His retreat, sheltered from storms, remained green the year round, and enabled him to gather about him a fine herd of cattle from the passing emigrant. His cattle finally became so numerous, that he drove them off to California, and returned with a splendid lot of horses. These, unfortunately,

tempted the cupidity of his Mormon neighbors, and he suddenly and mysteriously died.
The property was seized under some pretense,
and eventually distributed among the authorities of the church; and the poor squaw, with
three or four bright little half breeds, in a
state bordering on starvation, found shelter
in one of the caves which abound in these
cañons, her brief dream of happiness with the
white man brought rudely to a close.

The next day we passed a hot spring, directly by the roadside, which would be a curiosity in any other part of the world. The
water poured forth in a generous quantity,
forming a large marshy place, and coated
everything thickly with ferruginous matter—
the stones and earth were as red as blood. The
water itself was perfectly limpid, but salt and
very bitter. The upper side of the road was
lined with huge granite boulders, some of
them rising twenty feet high, and giving an
air of wildness to the scene. That night we
camped on another lovely spot. It was a
gravelly slope, which seemed to have been
formed by waters rushing from the small

cañon, at the mouth of which we took up our temporary abode. A clear, pebbly stream now issued forth, and the slope was covered with white primrose, lichnis, and wild geranium.

The next day we passed a collection of warm springs, all more or less salt; and near them was one of those large fountains which form the head of a considerable stream. The water poured out a heavy volume, and looked so clear that we were tempted to quench our thirst, just then at fever heat, but one taste of the briny fluid was enough—the lake itself was not more salt. Our day's journey brought us to within five miles of Bear river, on an uninteresting spot—a perfectly dead flat, the mountain rising abruptly from its surface—the animals, however, found good pasture, and that amply compensated for the tameness of the scenery.

To-day has been a noted one in our journey. We have passed the Bear and Malad rivers, and are now encamped on the banks of the latter stream. I hope we have not many more such crossings to encounter. Bear river is bounded by bluffs about fifty feet high, very steep, descending which brought us upon a narrow flat, forming the valley of the stream. The river itself is about two hundred feet wide, a deep, swift, turbid, and gloomy current, forming a fit boundary to the Mormon empire. We found a rough, crazy-looking ferry-boat; and the ferryman, sufficiently Charon-like for this modern Styx, was ready to land us on the western side for a consideration. The cattle were first driven in, and swam across; and here occurred an incident that frightened me not a little. One pair of oxen were carried below the landing place, and not being able to climb up the steep bank, rolled over each other, twisting their necks in the yoke, and there was a fair prospect of one or both being drowned. Morse plunged in to save them, and, it seemed to me, he came near being drowned, too; but "all's well that ends well." Our mules were driven on to the boat; but, when it started from the shore, the stupid things kept backing until they went in backwards, and, after being rescued, had to be stripped of their harness and driven through like the cattle. The carriages and the human chattels, not having the fear of the flood before them, were safely ferried across.

After our carriage had been taken over, and I had quietly seated myself out of the sun's rays, Mr. Livingston rode up with the mail, and, oh joy of joys! there was a batch of letters from home. Of course, I soon forgot Bear river, and all connected with it, and was "over the hills and far away." If ever I get home again, and have friends simple enough to be wandering in the Great Basin, or any other outlandish part of creation, I now promise to be a faithful correspondent. No one can describe the intense pleasure of receiving "letters from home," under such circumstances; nor is there anything to which I can compare it, unless it be that of one in a burning fever, who dreams of quenching his raging thirst at a cool and limpid fountain.

Three or four miles further brought us to the next obstacle, the Malad, bounded by similar bluffs. This appears, usually, to be a mere creek, but it was high water, and the space between the bluffs was completely flooded. It is a very sluggish stream, but occasioned us a world of trouble to get over—the wagons and carriages having to be unloaded to save their contents from a wetting. Ourselves, with all the goods and chattels of the train, were taken over by piece-meal, in a light, portable boat, which has been provided for such emergencies—a rope being stretched from bank to bank as a guide. Once over, everything had to be reloaded, making the operation similar to a house-moving on the first of May, by those poor mortals who are unable to live in a tenement of their own. The space between the bluffs is thickly lined with reeds, and the true bed of the stream may be easily traced by their absence. Here we are encamped on the western bank, on a disagreeable clay soil, rendered wet and muddy by the dripping cattle as they emerge from the water. Every one is tired and weary of the day's operations, and I feel so, too, because the rest are.

10*

LETTER XIV.

FROM BEAR TO MARY'S RIVER.

VALLEY OF THE HUMBOLDT, June 3d, 1855.

I BEGIN to think the Great Basin, like many other great things in this world, a great humbug. I had become impressed, as have, doubtless, many others, that this geographical wonder was surrounded on all sides by an immense circular range of mountains as a rim, after surmounting which, would be found a hollow or basin, in which there were comparatively few obstacles to locomotion. But this is altogether a mistake. Thus far it has been a labyrinth of mountains, irregular highlands, frightful gorges, very interesting to the geologist and geographer, but dreadfully wearisome to the traveler, as we can vouch. We have passed I don't know how many summits, and found streams running to all points of the compass. We have Fremont's map, and by its aid have tried to keep up a knowledge of our whereabouts; but are compelled to rely much more upon Capt. Egan, who pronounces the map inaccurate.

We are now encamped near the head of the valley of the Humboldt, or Mary's river, for two or three days, until an exploring party can return. It seems the swollen state of the river has rendered the usual road, which runs mostly on the north side, nearly impassable; and the prospect now is, that we may be compelled to make a track for ourselves, over the bluffs, on the south side. At any rate, I take advantage of the delay in putting together the scattered fragments of my journal, that you may have an account of things heard and seen, since we left the Malad on the 10th of May, nearly a month ago.

Our first day's journey was only three miles, owing to the tired state of the men and animals; but this brought us to a beautiful green slope, covered with blue-bottles and other flowers—and to the South stretched far away the valley of the Lake, the whole extent of which, about one hundred and eighty miles, was open to view, bounded by snowy ranges.

Our position was a commanding one, inasmuch as we could plainly trace the Bear and Malad winding to their junction, and to the Lake; and the white shores of the latter, incrusted with salt sparkled in the sun; and the islands, some tame and others rising into rocky peaks, dotted this sea of salt, and made up a combination of grand and beautiful, rarely to be found. We were directly north of an arm or bay of the Lake, formed by a high promontory which run a great distance south. The large cattle train of Halliday & Warner, rival merchants at the city, were a little in advance. At evening their camp fires flickered in the darkness, and we could distinguish figures moving to and fro, though too distant for sounds to reach us—fancy gave them the appearance of spectres.

Our route along the northern end of the Lake, through a depression of the highlands which formed the promontory, over a rough up-and-down road, giving us an occasional glimpse of the water, did not possess many striking features. One day we descended into a valley, some fifteen miles broad, having a stream running to the north, and whether it swept around and emptied into Bear river, or was a confluent of the waters of Oregon, we could not determine; but if the latter we were out of the Great Basin, so called.

We encamped one night on the slope forming the western bounds of the valley, and enjoyed an extended prospect. The soil was sandy, and a fierce wind whirled it in eddies around us, seasoning our dinner rather too highly for comfort. The cattle spread themselves over an immense range in search of food; and just at evening three well-formed savages rode into camp, mounted and armed, staid a short time, peered about with great inquisitiveness, and then rode off at top speed, disappearing over the hills at the northwest. The movement was suspicious: in a few minutes two or three mounted men sped in the same direction, and shortly after the herd were seen gathering from different points of the compass, for the purpose of being guarded for the night. To me the scene was wild and exciting; and I could not help anticipating our dreams might be rudely disturbed by a band of whooping Indians, in quest of our animals, if not bent on more tragic mischief. The night passed quietly off, however, with no other commotion than that occasioned by the wind, which did not abate its fury, and rendered the next day's travel uncomfortable.

The highlands exhibited a scattered growth of stunted pine and cedar—each tree forming a clump branching out from the bottom, with a rounded outline nearly in the shape of a hay stack, and rising not much higher. In a grove of these trees we found the train of Halliday & Warner, encamped for a few days, and in which our old traveling companions, Mr. and Mrs. Phelps, were making their way to California. At this point, Dr. H.'s wagon very opportunely broke down, and detained us, while repairing, long enough to make Mrs. P. a visit. I found her suffering with her old enemy, the chills. The baby, poor thing, has commenced the journey of life roughly, and needs more care than it can possibly receive. By the side of their traveling habitation, were a French family in one of the huge wagons composing the train. The daughter, a very pretty girl, descended the steps lightly, and led forth several domestic fowls for their daily exercise, while the father, grimly bearded, was anxiously watching an omelette in the spider —the mother quietly looking on. I asked the old lady how she carried these chickens, seeing no fixture in the wagon for that purpose.

"Oh, in the wagon, indeed—and they behave like leetle ladeès—never speak—lay every day—don't even cackle for fear of disturbing us—*Ma chere amie*—they know I'm talking of them now."

Sure enough, the "*leetle ladees*" waddled about and peered at us, knowing enough to make good the boast of their mistress.

The young miss, however, manifested less interest in her charge, than in being seen by the beaux of the camp, who were galloping about, California fashion. Mrs. P. said she had already refused several of them, and intimated that she was reserving herself for an easy victory over some wealthy inhabitant of the gold region.

Leaving our friends, we found ourselves comfortably camped near a range of hills, south

of us, on a fine grassy slope, a noisy stream
of water roaring and dashing to the northwest,
as though impatient to reach its journey's end.
Here we found some beautiful white marble,
also handsome specimens of laminated mica.
In the enthusiasm of the moment, we generally gather up such geological trophies as
strike our fancy, but, in the end, are compelled
to throw them away on account of the weight.
Does this stream pay tribute to the sluggish
waters of Salt Lake, to be carried off by evapo-
ration, or is it hurrying on to the ocean
through the waters of Oregon? The latter
we believe to be the fact, especially as the
next stage brought us to a deep, swift stream,
called, by the Captain, De Cassure Creek,
which flows still more directly north. It was
so narrow that it seemed as though we might
almost step from one bank to the other; yet
so deep that we were compelled to use our
boat, and undergo the unloading and loading
process, as at the Malad.

After crossing, our route was southwesterly,
and the next day's ride brought us into the
Fort Hall road, and past the Steeple Rocks.

These rocks are well named, consisting of four
steeples or pinnacles, which shoot up, one
much higher than the rest, and look as though
they might be the towers of a ruined castle
of feudal times. I suppose a machinist, in
these utilitarian times, would fancy them the
chimneys to some vast forge, in which Vulcan
was the master workman, in by-gone days.
Soon after passing these towering rocks, we
descended into a pleasant valley, at the western side of which rose up the Goose Creek
mountains. In this valley, on the banks of a
small, quiet stream, we took up our habitation,
and spent a whole week waiting for the cattle
purchased by Mr. L. at Bridger's, and which
were to join us from the Fort Hall road at
this point.

A week's residence in camp, in a traveling
caravan, is a dreadfully dull business, however
much the scenery may combine of the grand
and beautiful. Here was a broad valley, at
least five miles in width, stretching away
southeasterly and northwesterly, as far as the
eye could reach; in front were summits covered with snow; huge rocks were piled up

in towering majesty, commanding admiration; flowers were thickly scattered along banks of the creek, modestly wasting their sweets upon the desert air; yet, in less than a single half day, the whole scene began to pall upon the sight. The truth is, in traveling, the interest can only be kept up by continual locomotion—each day presenting its new scenes of beauty or grandeur.

We soon became domesticated in our transient residence. Our camp extended along the margin of the little stream at least a fourth of a mile, and established its "up town and down town" distinctions. Before this, Mrs. Kinney's arrangements were completed, and we had settled down into a regular kind of migratory house-keeping; and, really, we fare about as well, and have matters as orderly, as in a first class hotel. There seems to be nothing wanting but a first and second bell as a summons to our meals. The fare is excellent. Breakfast—beef steak, white trout, from Utah Lake, slightly salted, eggs and coffee, with an abundance of cream: and soup, roast beef, with puddings and preserved fruits, with variations, form the dinner. A large and convenient tent is pitched on the halting of the train, and our hospitable host presides with as much attention as though we were temporary visitors. He contends there is no reason why we should not live as well in camp as elsewhere; and as there are plenty of cows in the herd to be milked, and of fat beeves to be slaughtered, the means of generous fare are abundantly at hand.

After the first day we took one or two short excursions, something like a mile from head quarters; but fresh Indian signs were discovered, and it was not deemed prudent to venture any further. The same day, towards evening, one of the horses came rushing in, trembling in every joint, as though a band of red skins were in full chase. Men were sent in haste to gather the rest, and, particularly, to look after the safety of Rob Roy, the pet horse of the camp, the favorite of Mr. L., and really a beautiful and intelligent animal; and, soon after, the cattle came bounding in. It is a grand sight, the gathering of this great herd for guarding during the night

—almost equal to a band of buffalo—lowing, bellowing, and rushing madly about, with any number of mock fights and playful tiltings with each other; and, occasionally, some hundreds rush wildly on together in a kind of stampede, shaking the very ground beneath their feet. Sometimes our carriage is completely hemmed in by huge oxen, almost the size of elephants, and we are compelled to make a grand flourish of whips to prevent mischief. The calves, too, in the melée, would be separated from their mothers; and, like other juveniles, under similar trying circumstances, made their share of the noise. On these occasions, Kinney makes himself useful in attending to their wants.

Notwithstanding the usual dullness of camp life, each day brought with it some matter of interest. One day, with great labor, we climbed to the top of a high peak, on which rested a few wasting snow-banks; and had a fine view of a snowy range to the northwest, evidently in Oregon. We found a wilderness of huge granite boulders—plenty of mica schist and aricacious quartz—and also some stratified

rocks. Of course, we are on the look out for
precious stones—expect to find a few diamonds, and any number of rubies and sap-
phires, not to mention less attractive minerals.
Among the curiosities of the animal kingdom,
we discovered and captured a horned toad—
a singular-looking object, truly—the horns, instead of projecting from its head in a civilized
way, proceed, in small points, from its sides,
like the teeth of a saw.

At evening the clouds rolled up from the
mountains, and burst upon us in a heavy storm.
The lightning was exceedingly vivid, and the
thunder growled and crashed around us with
terrible energy. Our carriage rocked in the
wind, but kept up its old water-tight reputation, and we were as snug as heart could wish,
all things considered. But the poor cattle
turned their backs to the tempest and rushed,
in a body, to the opposite highlands; and the
men had to turn out and chase them for miles,
before they succeeded in bringing back the
runaways.

On the 20th, while at dinner, a long train
came winding around the hill from the direc-

tion of Steeple Rocks, and stretched itself across the valley. In the stillness and absence of life in this mountain vale, the moving of such a body in the distance, without so much as the sound of a whip, or the everlasting " gee-up-whoa," seemed more like a phantasm of the imagination than living beings. Two of the men branched off, and rode up to greet us, from whom we learned that it was the train of Halliday & Warner, as we had conjectured. A magnificent sunset closed the day, soft and beautiful, lighting up the thunder clouds at the north, tinging with gold their distinct and massy outlines; and the deep booming which came forth from that direction, told of a storm passing around us.

The next day a train, with a great drove of sheep, said to number four thousand, en-camped near us. They belong to a Mr. Goodell, an old mountaineer; and he has large Span-ish dogs, and a motley band of men, consisting of swarthy Mexicans, and Indians of various tribes—there was also a Lipan, and one or two Pinos from the interior of New Mexico, with a number of thieving, murdering Comanches, exhibiting a marked difference in physiognomy—altogether a very vagabond-looking train. Goodell hails from our own State; has a wife, it is said, in every tribe of natives with whom he has traded, for the sake of the influence which it gives him; wears richly-worked buckskin pants and moccasins, evincing a degree of taste and neatness in his squaw tribes superior to the eastern tribes; and a gaudy belt around his waist, garnished with weapons, giving him the appearance of a finished mountain rover. He is emphatically a monarch in his dominions, whips his ragged group for the least insubordination, and they obey his slightest glance, as he lies dreamingly smoking upon his bed of skins. He expects to make a fabulous sum out of his long-legged, coarse-wooled, black-nosed animals, looking very different from our mild, innocent, dumpling-shaped sheep. We visited his flock, and he pointed out to us, as a great curiosity, one that had four horns.

On the 23d, the rest of the train came up, making an addition of about six hundred, mostly cows, to our already large herd; and the next day we joyfully ended our week's sojourn, making our way over the mountains, through a pass which seems to have been made on purpose. The ascent was not very steep, but we found melting snow banks and plenty of mud. Remnants of broken wagons were scattered along; and among other evidences of the perseverance and energy of the white race, were the rusted shafts, wheels, and other machinery for a steam mill, left here in 1849, on which some unfortunate emigrant had founded his hopes of a fortune in the western El Dorado. Stern, indeed, must have been the necessity which compelled the owner to leave it, after overcoming two-thirds of the distance from the States—a thing to be gazed at in wonder by the Indians.

We soon passed over the snow beds, and, as we emerged from the pass, after reaching the summit, exclamations were heard from all, on the wild grandeur and beauty of the scene. Heavy thunder clouds enveloped some distant peaks, giving them the appearance of active volcanos rolling up dense volumes of smoke;

while the stratified hill sides, in our more immediate vicinity, abounded in rich coloring, purple and crimson predominating, on a base of soft green, changing and shifting as a light mist rose and fell. It was among the unrivaled panoramic views with which we are favored. We rested under two or three spreading, stunted cedars, near the summit, to enjoy the prospect, in a spot where weary ones, bound to California, had wept bitter tears—a few graves, the scattered fragments of wagons, and the bones of dead animals, furnished abundant and speaking evidence of their sufferings. This journey is only for those who have health and spirits to enjoy and to endure: to those who are unfortunate, it is a chapter of woe.

We finally rolled, tumbled, and pitched, I hardly know how, down, down, until we safely landed on a swiftly-running and noisily-roaring branch of Goose Creek. In some of the worst places the mules would seem to fold up their slender legs, and slide down on their haunches with a knowing look, as though that was the only way to keep the carriage from performing a somerset over their heads.

11

The party, consisting of Mr. L., Dr. H., and
ourselves, halted on the banks of the stream
to wait for the rest of the train; and I must
confess I looked anxiously at the thick growth
of willows, and the huge granite boulders, not
knowing what moment an arrow would whiz
into our group. Soon, however, to my relief,
the advance squad of cattle came bounding
down the declivities, a welcome sight; and,
after crossing the stream, we found a cosy
camping place : a complete basin, surrounded
by jagged highlands, covered with a scrubby
growth of cedar. Bright tufts of crimson flowers were thickly scattered over the rocky dé-
bris. Our tent was pitched on a natural lawn,
where nothing but the finest, softest grass
grew : if it had been clipped and rolled for
years, it could not have been more velvety.
We walked to the top of the nearest hill,
while the train was gathering and folding up
its huge length. The sight was imposing—
the scouts hurried about here and there,
searching every nook and corner, with their
guns gleaming in the descending sun, not
for enemies, but poor, simple cows and

calves. I fancied we were a tribe of wandering Scythians, that this spot was now all the world to us, and that ere long we should go forth in search of other green pastures.

I am sure our descent was much longer than our ascent on the other side of the mountain; and, as the water flows northwesterly, we must have been in a deep valley, descending towards Oregon.

We kept on descending until we came to Goose Creek, up which our route lay southwesterly. A parallel range of mountains, apparently some forty to fifty miles from the one we had just surmounted, forms an immense valley, the filling up of which consists of passes, cañons, gorges, and a multitude of lateral streams; we passed any number of the latter, some of which, muddy and miry, we floundered through with difficulty—narrowly escaping a disagreeable application of hydropathy. In one place a monad-shaped hill stood solitary and alone, on a level piece of ground, the side facing the road nearly perpendicular, and at the top a strata of rocks, extending at least the fourth of a mile, so even that it seemed a work of art. In another place, for more than a mile, the bluffs on our left were lined with soft limestone rocks, shelving over and scooped into all manner of shapes—ovens and miniature caves—into one or two of which our gentlemen had the curiosity to creep. As these cavities are sheltered from the weather and floods, it is difficult to see how they could have been produced, unless the bluffs have, at some time, been the shore of a large body of water, and the soft parts of the rock washed out by the dashing waves. Large quantities of marl also made their appearance from time to time, ready to dispense their riches to some future agriculturists.

On the 26th we left the immediate valley of Goose Creek, following up one of its branches through a narrow pass, lined with scoria and basaltic rocks. Singular specimens of isolated rocks, some of great height, and others of fantastic shape and figure, stood up like ancient heroes, turned into stone while fighting their last battle. We wound our way through in a very tortuous manner, crossing and recrossing

the brawling stream continually. After passing another cañon, scorched and blackened by
volcanic fires, like the throat of a furnace, and
up a stony ascent, we found a camping place
by the side of a little gurgling brook, covered
with luxuriant grass, to the great delight of
the cattle, many of which, however, were
soon floundering in treacherous quicksands.
Flowers, of every hue and delightful fragrance,
were in abundance; and so we go on from
desolation to fertility, which strangely alter-
nate throughout this whole region—now a
sterile defile, blackened with volcanic fires,
and then a lovely vale, clothed in the very
luxury of vegetation.

The next day we passed a summit, the
waters evidently running southwesterly. Do
they find a passage through the range on our
left, into Salt Lake, or through the Humboldt,
into the Mary's River? Geographers have yet
much to learn of the Great Basin.

The same day we came into "Thousand
Spring Valley," and encamped in a small
lateral cañon, near one of the most beautiful
springs of clear, cold water I ever beheld—

gushing out from under a limestone rock, and
running over clean gravel, some distance,
before reaching a grassy level. Opposite to
us were the remains of a few wretched lodges
of the Utahs, constructed of wild sage bushes;
and they had managed partly to burrow in the
hill side during the past winter. Broken arrow
heads of obsidian, remnants of rudely-fashioned
baskets for catching fish, and snow shoes, were
scattered about : the dens of wild beasts could
scarcely have furnished less evidence of civilization. Fresh tracks indicated the near presence of the savages, and our captain was
on the *qui vive* against a surprise. Several
new varieties of flowers, with primrose and
cactus, rewarded the short walk we were permitted to make from camp.

The next day—the Sabbath—our course was
westerly, up Thousand Spring Valley, over
ground strongly impregnated with alkali—the
pools by the wayside filled up by a recent
storm, exhibiting the appearance of common
lye. In passing a low, wet spot we got into
trouble : Mr. L. was in front, and his strong,
heavy horses floundered through ; while our

mules, immediately in the rear, plumped down to their necks in the mud, as though it were a matter of course—the carriage sinking, too, up to the axle-trees, as fixed and immovable, apparently, as fate. Here was a fix. Our animals, after a few struggles, gave the matter up very quietly, and pointed forward their ears in admiration, as though they felt themselves the "observed of all observers." The audience was small, but decidedly interested. How we were to be extricated I could not see; but Mr. L. encouraged us by representing it as a trifling predicament.

In the first place, the mules were relieved of their harness; and, one at a time, with a little assistance, wallowed through, covered with saline mud of the color of ashes, in a very sorry plight. After breaking all the lariats, and partly miring Mr. L.'s team in a vain attempt to draw out the carriage rearward, Canfield, one of the Mormon missionaries, who is on his way to California, came up with a yoke of oxen, and drew us from the miry pit. I thought we might have made a fair tableau for one of the scenes in the

Diorama of Pilgrim's Progress, though it is hardly fair to allow Canfield—who is most irreverently called "Old Si," as a contraction for Cyrus—to represent Great Heart. It seems we had taken one of the branching roads, which had been disused on account of the treacherous nature of the soil, and the train passed us to the right, near the bluffs. Soon after overtaking the train, we encountered the principal stream of the valley, deep and rapid, and were compelled to use our portable boat, and once more unload the wagons. It was a Sabbath most wearisomely spent; and, in this respect, strongly contrasted with the quiet and peaceful aspects of the day in civilized lands.

The next day we continued our course westerly up a small, clear, gravelly stream, which finally led up a beautiful grassy ravine, in the mountain range, we had been continually approaching. About half way in the ascent, we found a level place, so well abounding in grass near a spring that the Captain, contrary to the usual custom, concluded to halt at mid-day, and refresh man and beast. While cosily seated around our well-supplied table, we had, for the first time since leaving the north end of Salt Lake, a visit from the natives—five or six Shoshonies, as they claimed to be. They had good-natured countenances, and were better formed and dressed than we expected to see on this route. Two of them stood near, and made laughing remarks to each other, wondering that so much ceremony should be necessary, and occasionally pointing to the roast beef upon the table, and then to his mouth, saying, "*tick-up, tick-up*," which means "I'm hungry."

We continued ascending on a pleasant road, occasionally shaded by a handsome growth of trees—a great rarity in this part of the world—until we reached the summit. From this point the view was magnificent. In front, some fifteen miles distant, was a portion of the veritable Humboldt range, clothed in snow; a part glittering in the sun, and another part enveloped in a heavy thunder cloud, which gave out muttering evidences of a storm. In a northerly direction we had a view of the snowy mountains of Oregon, over which hung another portentous bank of clouds, black as

11*

night, and gleaming with frequent flashes of lightning. A thunder storm is always a grand spectacle, but it transcends description when rolling and flashing over these mighty elevations, as though such were the scenery where its sublimity can be appropriately displayed.

We waited until the rest of the train came up, and then descended for some miles into a wide, pleasant, grassy valley, when, it becoming evident we were to encounter the storm, the Captain gave the welcome order for encamping. We had scant time to make the necessary preparation, before the tempest broke upon us in great fury. The lightning seemed to envelop us in perfect sheets of flame, and the thunder crashed and pealed over us, at a rate beyond all former conception. The rain came down in torrents, and, as our carriage rocked in the blast, it seemed as if we must be swept off like so much thistle down; yet the thick, close covering kept us as dry as in a house, and, in an hour's time, the sun came smilingly out, as though the face of nature never intended again to put on a frowning aspect.

The next morning we had another visit from the natives, and, to our utter surprise, they gave notice that one of the cattle had been left in the rear: they cannot be so wholly bad after all. One of them was dressed in a complete suit of the white man, obtained, as the men insisted, by robbery or murder. I asked him—partly by signs, and partly by words—whether he would kill a white man, if in his power; he opened his jacket, and, pointing to his heart, said: "American kill Shoshonee." In passing through the valley, we had more or less of the natives with us all day, and saw their "*wick-ee-ups*" at different points in the distance, made up of grass and sage bushes—some of the grass ones woven very neatly, presenting the appearance of large bee-hives. The valley deepened as we proceeded, and, to all appearance, extended to a great distance on the east of the Humboldt range; but a sudden turn to the right through a pass, brought us to a pleasant camping ground on a rivulet flowing into Mary's River, only a mile or two from us. The mail-carrier came in from California, with a dismal account of the roads and the mosquitos—the former, along the river, next to impassable; and the latter, of superior size and industry, were his daily and nightly torment. The train of Halliday & Warner had just crossed the river, and in so doing had encountered serious difficulties; and another train in advance of that had spent four days in crossing a small stream.

Under these circumstances, Captain Egan concluded to keep on the south of the river. We went on about seven miles, and here we now are, encamped on the bluffs — a clear stream rushing past us from the mountains to the left, its banks thickly bordered with bright orange lupins of unusual size; and the ground, in patches, carpeted with moss pink. The Captain and four men have gone forward to explore; the weather is a drizzly rain, and, though I can keep dry by remaining housed in our traveling mansion, it shuts off some pleasant walks that might be made along the creek in search of flowers. The men, yesterday, caught a brood of sage chickens, so shy that they sit with their eyes closed when you are looking at them; but their cry for the old bird was so mournful, that I let them go this morning. A party with pack mules, from California, came in from the main road to obtain a supply of flour—a dreadfully rough looking set of men—and they confirm the news of the river route being flooded. We begin to believe the Indians, who continue to say— "*Pe-op, Ca-wino*," which Morse translates, "water no good."

June 4. Last evening our commander returned after exploring fifty miles of the route, and reports it entirely practicable, with plenty of grass and water. We are to keep close to the mountains, on account of more easily crossing the streams; and the ox teams are to constitute our van-guard, to break through the everlasting sage bushes and grease wood, which constitute the ornamental shrubbery of this region. To-day is spent in preparation, and to-morrow we commence a route destined to be called "Egan's Cut Off." Some fine trout from the stream have been added to our good cheer, resembling our far-famed brook trout in shape, but of richer coloring, the crimson spots being a deep purple.

LETTER XV.

WASSAW VALLEY, July 10, 1853.

ROB, the favorite horse of Mr. L., and decidedly the pet of the whole camp, can do
almost everything, but talk outright in human
fashion; and he has ways of expressing himself
which no one can misunderstand. I never saw
a more beautiful animal. He seems to be perfectly aware that he is a privileged being;
every other horse gives way to him; and as
to the mules, poor humble things, he has only
to turn his head with a peculiar leer, and they
hurry off as though they expected to be annihi-
lated. His skin is as soft and silky as satin,
under the daily grooming of Kinney; and he is
fed with sundry knick-knackeries by everybody.
He is fond of sugar, and, time and again, I

have fed him with it from my hand; and it is curious to see with what delicate care he will lick it off without hurting me. He comes regularly to our carriage for crackers and odd ends of biscuit; and if the door happens to be shut he will rub against it; and, sometimes, when I do not notice him, he will take hold and give my dress a slight pull to attract attention, and often lay his nose in my lap like a dog. Marvelous stories are told of his performances. Once he saved his master's life, by bearing him bravely through the flood in the Missouri—and, again, he distanced a band of mounted savages, running nearly a whole day and part of the night. No wonder he is a favorite.

We had another camp pet worthy of mention. In passing a place where Goodell had encamped the previous night, a little lamb was discovered in the sage bushes—the poor little thing had been left in the confusion. Its cries were piteous, and it was carefully put into one of the wagons, and has been brought along and taken care of; and it is pleasant to witness the interest which the roughest men in the train take in the welfare of the little cast-away.

On the 5th of June, in a clear, chilly atmosphere, we resumed our journey. After going up stream for more than a mile to find a crossing, and then filling our water cans with the pure cold water, for emergencies, we made our pathless way along the base of the mountains, through sage bushes, now rough, now smooth, interspersed with patches of beautiful flowers. The marked features of the day were the swift streams we were compelled to cross; some more impetuous than Niagara's rapids—and all that enabled us to stem the current was, the impetus obtained in going down the precipitous banks; the leaders plunging in with a bound, and the men on the lower side shouting and swinging their arms to keep them from turning their heads down stream.

Our wheels passed over brilliant beds of lupins—a metallic blue and pink predominating. A showy crimson scarlet honeysuckle, with a singular rose semi-double, were the new flowers of the day's ride. Some fairy dells opening into the icy range on the left, with green slopes, soft and warm looking, carpeted with bright flowers—a torrent foaming down in the midst, lined with cotton wood and quaking aspen—make the prettiest views imaginable. With the aid of a glass we saw Halliday's train across the river, just extricating themselves from its slimy banks, after a week's durance. We encamped near the base of one of the mountain benches, the cold air of the morning changed to an insupportable sultriness, with a torment of mosquitos; but, at evening, the breeze from the snow tops was delightfully refreshing.

June 6. The morning fair, and we leave camp in fine spirits. This mountain air is like exhilarating gas, and we feel like mounting upwards, when, lo! we are stopped by a swift stream, and our Pegasus-like ardor clipped of its wings. The banks were unusually steep and precipitous; the creek larger than usual, and lined with cotton wood and small bushes, through which a pathway was hewn. The water rushed and roared among the granite boulders, lashing itself into fury, as though

impatient that its precincts should be invaded
by the footsteps of the pale faces. Down,
down we rush; in plunge the animals, the
water surging, for a moment, over the very
backs of the leaders—then, hurrah with crack-
ing whips and shouts, we rush madly through,
raked by the overhanging branches; and then,
thank heaven, we emerge on the opposite side,
and breathe freely again. A slight deviation,
pulling of the wrong rein, striking of a wheel
against a large boulder, or other mischance,
would have wrecked us. One of the carriages,
in the confusion, was turned down stream and
upset, and a young man by the name of Phelps
rescued with difficulty; and it was two hours'
work to get the vehicle from the water.

These bounding water-courses are generally
lined with trees. At first it was a welcome
sight; these trees stretching from the mountain down into the valley, as far as the eye
could reach—thinly scattered, to be sure—
nevertheless, green trees contrasting pleasantly
with bare rocks and other forms of desolation.
But we begin to regard a belt of trees as an
indication that we have a difficult crossing

before us. Another annoyance, too, besets us, in the mosquitos and buffalo gnats, which come out from the foliage in perfect clouds, and manifest an importunity of hunger that will take no denial. The men break off boughs and flourish them around their heads—I find a veil invaluable. A few Diggers made their appearance and looked ugly and malicious.

We encamped at evening on the banks of a deep and rapid stream, flowing from an extended valley in the Humboldt mountains, which we at first supposed to be the south fork of the Mary's River. The next morning we went up stream some distance, to find a crossing. Capt. Egan's countenance and speech have the usual non-committalism of other leaders; but I detected in his looks, that we had a difficult task before us. The banks were spaded down to make the descent a little more easy, and then the various vehicles were dragged through by a long train of oxen, until the soft, spongy soil became so cut up, that it was impossible to get in or out without upsetting. The first capsize was the flour wagon; but so slight was the immersion, that the sacks were soon dried. The next one contained several of the men, and, among the rest, Dr. Coward, who emerged from his bath very much alarmed. To his terror succeeded rage, and, being something of a cockney, the company were made good-humored, in the midst of their troubles, by the maledictions which he poured out; first on himself for being idiot enough to leave London; and next, on Old England for being the mother of such a " *dom*" country, in which a gentleman could not pass a stream without danger of being drowned. He opened his traveling bag, and his anathemas increased in intensity as he pulled forth each dripping garment. The last I saw of him he was interceding with Mrs. Kinney to restore the collars and shirt bosoms into presentable shape for Sacramento, where he intends to make his début, as "Surgeon from Queen's Hospital, London."

The landscape, pleasantly rolling towards the river in easy descent, was varied by occasional belts of cotton wood. In one tree, of better size, we espied an eagle's nest, with two or three of the king of birds flying high over us. We passed acres and acres, literally covered with brilliant lupins, standing up two feet high, very beautiful and fragrant. Sage bushes in abundance, and in places huddled up in the form of an oven, from which the miserable Diggers fled on our approach. Some four or five made their appearance suddenly, as though they had sprung from the ground, and disappeared just as mysteriously. Evening found us on a broad, grassy plateau, with plenty of flowers, near a deep cavity, filled with trees and willows, and a noisy creek dashing through. Men were sent out scouring every nook and corner, to guard against an ambuscade, and a few savages in the camp were deprived of their arms and placed under guard until morning, not forgetting, however, as an equivalent for this durance, to satisfy their hunger.

In the morning I anticipated another difficult crossing; but was agreeably surprised to find a safe bridge, which the men had found time to construct. Some half dozen Indians followed us all day. After dashing through a number of creeks, some miry, others rocky, with more or less of breakages, we finally came in sight of a heavier belt of timber than usual; and, soon, one of the men, sent forward to explore, returned with news of trouble ahead. Our course was directed nearer the mountains, and we kept ascending until we came to the mouth of the cañon from which the stream issues forth. It was pronounced to be four feet deep, and in swiftness exceeded all my conceptions of the rush of water—surging madly by; and, when it encountered a boulder too firmly imbedded to be swept along, it shot up jets like a geyser. The cañon was deep and rocky—its sides lined with huge patches of snow; and, higher up, we could see a portion of the glittering mantle which hung on the mountain summit.

Fortunately the banks were not precipitous. The animals were soon unharnessed, and picketed upon the rich carpet of grass, and all hands went to work to construct a bridge. I was the only idler in camp. In an incredibly short time, trees were cut down, and hauled up by ox teams—the timber thus prepared was extended across, and brush and

dirt thrown on, making a safe and ready pas-
sage-way.

In the mean time, eight or ten Diggers gathered about, watching, with much curiosity,
the felling of trees for string-pieces, having,
probably, never seen an axe in use before.
As the hours wore away, they became wearied
of gazing, and resorted to their daily avocation
of searching each other's tangled horse-hair
locks for the inhabitants, which they disposed
of in a way not very appetizing to the specta-
tor. The experiment of two Edinburgh sa-
vans in eating snails was fairly outdone. After
this exercise they sang, in a monotonous tone,
a few songs, keeping time with their whole
body, having short sticks in their hands which,
Morse says, they use for gambling. They
seemed like Arab dervishes, with their wild,
dreamy looks, as they sat swaying their bodies
to and fro. Suddenly, one of them sprang to
Dr. H. and begged his pipe, and, on being
refused, attempted to grasp it. I expected to
see a knife glitter, as the next salutation; but
the Western differs from the Eastern vagabond
in the fashion of his arms. Two of them came

to the carriage and peered about, saying
"white squaw wick-ee-up"—tried to have
some talk with them, but not succeeding very
well, motioned them off.

We passed over in safety at evening, and
made our bivouac on the south side, on a bluff
near two immense granite boulders. Our supper was late, and the light in the tent attracted
swarms of mosquitos, much to our discomfort;
but necessity knows no law. Clouds hovered
over the mountain summit in angry masses,
with frequent flashes of lightning and peals
of thunder, but the Storm Spirit passed us by
with a few spattering drops.

In the morning about a dozen savages, naked, except a few rags, and squalid, and filthy
to the last degree, seated themselves on the
boulders and watched our movements; several
of them had dogs leashed to their wrist, very
much resembling foxes. One of them acted
a piece of pantomine with Dr. H., much to
our amusement. He spatted his bare legs
with a comical grin, complained that the gnats
would bite in spite of the clay with which he
had plentifully besmeared himself, and invited

the Doctor to make a transfer of his pants.
On being refused, his countenance changed to
a malignant scowl; and the glances which they
exchanged with each other manifested anything but good-will.

During the day one of our scouts returned,
hurriedly, with the news that he had been
stopped by a band of natives in a small collection of trees, and we began to anticipate
an unpleasant encounter. Our numbers, however, must have looked too formidable for op-
position; for when we came up to the grove,
with two or three little rivulets running at
random among the trees, the only evidence
of life was the lively music of the meadow
lark, and the more quiet notes of a small finch.
You may ask if I have any fear. Not the
least—not even as much as I have sometimes
felt around the fireside at home. Egan uses
great caution. The Indians in camp, as I have
before said, are placed under guard for the
night; the cattle are herded close to us; the
horses and mules picketed still closer, and
no one moves a rod without arms. These pre-
cautions bring their annoyances. The cattle
12

will use the wagons for rubbing places; and, in the night, some huge ox scratching himself on the rim of the carriage wheel, we are awakened with the sensation that the earth is undergoing a regular quake. Some nights we are provokingly kept awake for hours in this way—the creatures even contending for a rub, and we often apprehend being quite overturned in the battle.

For days and days we had an abundance of bushes, about four or five feet high, with yellow blossoms on the limbs, something after the manner of the flowering almond, and with a fragrance like mignonnette.

Our course for the last two days has been nearly west, leaving the Humboldt to the left; and, on the 10th, after a pleasant descent, we came upon the true south fork of the Mary— a stream of many channels, wide, swift, and deep. Along the banks ran an old road— Hastings' cut-off—leading to the main river, which, on examination further down, proved to be too miry, and we were compelled to continue our own route. A mile up stream we found the main channel running over a fine, broad, gravelly bottom, which was easily forded. After this, was a wide stretch between the river and the bluffs, made up of quick-sand and water-courses, through which we were drawn by five or six yokes of cattle—wallowing their way somehow; engulphed part of the time so that scarcely more than their horns were visible—the drivers in not much better plight, but still able to use the whip, and give their unearthly yells. It was painful to witness the desperate struggles of the poor animals through the black, oozing mud, and I was thankful enough to get over.

The day was nearly spent, and we established our quarters directly on the high bank, giving us an extended prospect of the country as it shelved in to form the valley of the river. It seemed to have been a favorite resort for the natives, as exhibited in the remains of small fires, broken arrow-heads, curiously fashioned from quartz and obsidian, and other mementoes of their presence. The sunset was splendid—surely there never were such rose-colored clouds, bordered with flames of purple and gold, as enveloped the snowy peaks of the

Humboldt—and there was, too, a clearness and depth to the sky, that it seemed as if the vision could penetrate its blue curtain into a region beyond the confines of matter.

We were congratulating ourselves on acheiving a difficult crossing in safety, when we made the disagreeable discovery that our camping ground was a mere promontory, formed by another branch of the river, which poured down a deep and swift flood of water—an obstacle in our path, apparently more troublesome than the one we had just surmounted. We were actually caught in a fork of the south fork.

The next morning we were called to breakfast at four, and made diligent preparation for the severe labors of the day. The stream lay between high bluffs, was in a swollen state, and covered all the space between. An English sailor, by the name of Lee, swam over with the end of a rope in his mouth, and fastened it to the opposite bank, and ourselves and all our worldly goods were ferried over. The sun's rays were perfectly scorching, and I ventured to raise a parasol, but was cautioned not to move, as a capsize would be a serious matter. I have really shown myself so much of a heroine in difficult places, that I was in great danger of losing my reputation; but you know I never could bear the hot sun. The oxen struggled through with the large wagons, swimming over the deep spots—one upset and came near drowning the poor animals. One or two cows got tangled and confused in a thicket of willows and were drowned. Mr. L. takes all these disagreeables with the utmost coolness, not allowing a look to express his interest in the matter, while I cannot help feeling as troubled as though it was verily all my own.

By mid-afternoon we were all safely moored on the other side, and then came up a thunder-shower, which settled down into a cold drizzly rain; and our camping ground, trampled by the cattle, became almost a quagmire. Poor things, they had the worst of it, and finding no convenient place to lie down, they exercised themselves diligently at the carriage wheels.

June 11. A dismally cold, wet, chilly air

—snow falling on the heights near us—the temperature varies daily as we approach to or recede from the mountains. Continued our route in search of the river, through a cañon; then over cedar heights, fragrant with the crushed boughs that were cut off to allow us passage—musical, too, with a few birds, and bright with showy tufts of crimson flowers, which we find abundant on light sandy soils. Passing through a rich grassy valley, of some fifteen miles in width, we encamped near highlands, the suburbs of a snowy range, hoping to find the river road which crosses from the north to the south side, it is supposed, not far from our vicinity. The river, by the way, has become a myth—a regular humbug, as Dr. H. insists. He says there is no Mary's River, and that we are lost in an endless maze of cañons and hills, as hopelessly as the Flying Dutchman on the sea. The men, too, tired of making roads through impassable places, are almost in a state of mutiny, and think their troubles will all be over when they find the much-talked-of river.

Our camp was on a most beautifully clear,

pebbly stream, on which we picked up a fine specimen of chalcedony.

Sabbath, June 12. I manage to keep up a knowledge of the Sabbath, though—

"The sound of the church going bell
These valleys and rocks never heard:"

The morning cold and drizzly. We started about ten, but were compelled to stop, in a few miles, in a low bottom, wet and narrow, where the mules sank fetlock-deep in a black loam that would have rejoiced the heart of a horticulturist—the rain descending in torrents. Near by, on the bluffs, were two of the Diggers' best habitations—the grass woven with much ingenuity, and the tops well thatched. On looking in we found them vacated; but three or four miserable wretches soon came into camp, exchanging antelope skins with the men for cast off clothing; and a harlequin group they became, with tattered red shirts and crownless hats. On the addition of every rag they paraded around for admiration, grinning with delight.

The next morning our track continued for

some miles in the same ravine, from which we were finally extricated by a wearisome drag up a mountain—the wheels cutting deep into the soft red earth. In the ascent we picked up some fine specimens of cornelian. At the summit we were amply repaid for our toil by a prospect which extended into Oregon, and displayed, on all sides, numberless peaks and cañons—a high rocky pyramid to the left seemed to be the presiding genius of the rugged scenery. Will the steam whistle .ever reverberate among these mountains and cavities? Brother Jonathan usually begins by proposing impossibilities, and ends in performing them; but those who drag their slow length across the continent, as we have, may well doubt the fulfillment of these promises during the present generation.

Having reached a high position, the next business, according to the universal law of traveling, was to make a corresponding descent; so down we went, some three thousand feet (so they said), landing in a deep, narrow grassy cañon, with plenty of beautiful flowers, the last pitch of our descent so steep that the mules slid down on their haunches; and, just as we reached the bottom, and were about to unchain the wheels, the forward squad of cattle came bounding after us, and it was as much as the men could do to prevent a disagreeable stampede. This defile opened into a broad, pleasant valley, about two miles wide, in which we made our bivouac—the ground abundantly clothed with grass and flowers. Capt. Egan reported the river about five miles below, but utterly impracticable to make our way along its banks.

The next morning, in high spirits at the proximity of the river, we continued our route west, up a ravine, and had a toilsome ascent of over a mile. When we reached the top there appeared to be an endless succession of mountains, hills, and deep gullies, thrown together and jumbled up without order or regularity, as though the earth had once been a furiously boiling fluid, and suddenly hardened. Then down we went into another deep cavity, from which it seemed impossible to get out; but, after winding around and about, through a confusion of hills, we finally reached very

12*

high ground, and, at last, had a distinct view
of Mary's River to the southwest.

From the last elevation we made another
plunge, and, going over and through all manner of rough and rocky ground, we fairly
lodged and stuck fast in a narrow fastness—hills
rising precipitously on each side, and a stream
running in the middle. The guide had made
a mistake, and piloted the train into the wrong
ravine; and it seemed as though we could
neither go forward nor retreat. But there was
no help for it; the day was well spent, every
one was tired to death, and we were compelled
to stop for the night, where we could not find
a level spot to sit, stand, or sleep. The largest
portion of the cattle were herded a mile in the
rear, else we must all, man and brute, have
been packed together like a barrel of herring.
Had we been assailed by a determined band
of savages, we must inevitably have been cut
off. Capt. Egan dreaded an attack, and put
nearly all the men on guard, and aroused the
camp soon after midnight.

By cutting away a thicket of willows, and
removing a few boulders, a passage down the

ravine was effected; but we went from one rugged pass to another, seemingly without end, until, finally, the river burst upon our view in a broad valley below—a most welcome sight. But what an extent of water, overflowing its banks in patches, apparently some miles in width! On the opposite side was a long train, now seen, now hid by sand hills, with a cloud of dust. The glass soon identified it as Halliday's. Our teamsters felt all the excitement of a race. This train had three weeks the start, and here we were in a more favorable situation—this particular point being the usual crossing-place from the north to the south side. An easy descent brought us to the flat river-bottom, which proved to be perfectly dry; a short detour to the right, and we were on the margin of a swift, irregular stream—the water so strongly impregnated with alkaline salts as to be undrinkable, except under strong compulsion. But oh! what legions of long-bodied, large-winged flies—our carriage, inside and out, was blackened with them—we could not move without crushing them by the score. Fortunately they had no bite or sting, and only annoyed us by the sensation of being covered with insects.

We soon rounded a bold, bluffy promontory, and entered upon a broad basin, at the left of which was an opening, as though a large tributary flowed from that direction. In front there appeared to be a smooth, uninterrupted plain for fifteen or twenty miles. On we went, and soon reached a stream, about the color of hotel coffee, which ran *from*, instead of *to*, the river. This we forded with difficulty, when we were stopped by a man returning from an exploration, with the report that the plain was full of these off-shoots from the main channel. There was no help for it, except to regain the base of the hill, and take an extensive circuit to avoid the soft bottom; but it was late, and no grass for a long distance. We therefore encamped amid the sage bushes, hot, dry, and dusty, annoyed with mosquitos, and doubly annoyed with a vile wood-tick—a new and abominable plague. It was excessively disagreeable; and the reflection, that our poor animals had no better fare than to crop a supper from sage and grease wood, added to the discomfort.

The next morning we started at an early hour, and made a great sweep, to clear the difficulties that beset our path the day before. We soon entered upon a saleratus plain, as smooth and hard as a house-floor, over which we rolled in a very lively manner. This surface had been formed by water which had accumulated by the overflowing of the river, forming a temporary lake—collecting and receding each year, and depositing its annual supply of alkaline salts.

The ensuing day we journeyed around an immense bend in the river, over another extensive saleratus flat—the weather unbearably hot, and the plain dusty. The great curiosity of the ride were the whirling columns of dust, like water spouts, which rose up in the distance, at first scarcely perceptible, and then increasing in bulk and altitude, until they reached a great height. They moved gracefully, carried by the wind to the north, along the base of the opposite mountain, some standing perpendicular, and others having a slight inclination, and looked like dancing phantoms. As we neared the scene of these cotillions, the wind increased almost to a gale, and whistled the dust around us in clouds. That evening we encamped on a clean, sandy place, sparsely covered with sage bushes, among which were multitudes of slender lizards, gliding about like sprites. I had before seen these reptiles, but not in such numbers. They are beautifully colored, some with bright red spots; have long, slender tails; dart like a flash from one bush to another; and, after reaching cover, will put out their heads, and take a look at you with their little, piercing eyes.

On the opposite side of the river was Stony Point, famed for many a savage murder; and, as if to revive the recollection, the skull of an Indian was picked up near the tent, with a bullet hole through it. Many and profound were the speculations as to where, when, and how the catastrophe happened; and whether the fatal aim was given by the white man or the red, without any satisfactory conclusion.

In our journey down the river, the history of one day's ride is that of another. We had hot weather—plenty of mosquitos, lizards, horned toads, wood ticks, poor water—and, worse than all, the grass disappeared except at distant intervals, and we were compelled to make some forced marches to provide for the wants of our animals. ,

Just at evening, on the 19th, while encamped in one of the numerous lateral valleys of the river—the cattle almost hid in a paradise of pasture, and we battling in a purgatory of insects—a young Pi-Ute, about eighteen years of age, well formed and active, made his appearance, and proved to be the greatest curiosity of the whole journey. He was a perfect mimic. When he first came in he described cattle, horses, and mules, by a series of pantomime, in such a comical way, that he was greeted with shouts of laughter, which he echoed back with interest. His powers of imitation were perfectly wonderful. On being asked—"*Wick-ee-up, where?*" with a wave of the hand around the horizon, to signify that he was desired to point out where he lived, he would repeat "*Wick-ee-up, where?*" in precisely the same tone, and make the same motion with his hand: and so of every thing that was said to him. The oddity of the thing produced peals of laughter; and, as we kept on laughing, he would wait till each peal was finished, and then give a precise counterpart. Mr. F. tried to puzzle him, by repeating over long sentences, such as

"Oh for a lodge in some vast wilderness,
Some boundless contiguity of shade,"

in a mouthing, declamatory style, but he would roll it off with no seeming difficulty, and make the same gestures. Of course he became a decided favorite; the entertainment was too good not to be paid for, and he was soon comfortably fed and clothed. After the comic acting had partially ceased, he imitated the men in a more useful way, by gathering fuel, bringing water, etc. He appeared so good-natured and sprightly that I wanted to take him with us, but of course it was impracticable.

In the morning he returned with two or three of his kindred, who expressed their dissatisfaction in unmeasured terms, when they found the generosity of the camp had expended itself upon the lad. One of them gave a significant twitch at my dress, as an article to be "swapped" for his tattered buckskin pants.

On the 26th we reached the sink of the river—a large basin, somewhat circular, from ten to fifteen miles wide, and twenty-five to thirty long, bounded by hills. The portion at present dry is crusted over with saline substances, very similar in appearance to the ground, after a storm of sleet which has congealed. Over the flat, smooth, desolate surface, we kept on for about ten miles—the road, in places, slippery from the recently receding water—and took up our quarters at one o'clock. The wind, brisk from the northwest, increased to a gale before evening, whirling clouds of dust along the base of the hills. At our left lay the lake, bordered by a belt of deep green grass and bulrushes, upon which the animals were driven with difficulty—poor things, they mired almost to their bodies, and the high wind, growing colder and colder at evening, drove them for shelter to the carriages, around which they huddled, complaining all night.

In the morning we resumed the journey over the smooth, wintry-looking plain, steering for a point of the mountain fifteen miles distant, which, in the clear atmosphere, appeared as though it might be reached in an hour's walk. Less than half the distance brought us to the shore of the lake (free from rushes), a beautiful sheet of water, from two to five miles wide, with a gravelly beach: saw a pelican and plenty of ducks. At the junction of the road from the other side of the sink were two trading stations, consisting of slight tents, and supplied with some necessaries for passing trains—but, it was said, diluted whisky and brandy composed most of the stock. These establishments were at the foot of an elevation, composed of red sand-stone and basaltic columns, resting on a strata of gray rock, running up at least a thousand feet, of varied jags, points, and turrets, making a view altogether too fine to be desecrated by a brace of rum holes.

A sluggish stream, which the men called a slough, with scarce any perceptible current, led from the lake, and connects with Carson Lake—the amount of water forming no sort of comparison to that which flows in through

Mary's River, and it is said to be dry during part of the year. We passed on a mile, and encamped to prepare for the Forty-mile Desert, immediately in prospect, about which all manner of dismal stories are told.

At evening a carriage drove into camp with a Mr. Halliday, within a few days from San Francisco. He had been on a visit to the rival train, of which he is a large proprietor, and was then on his return. It was reviving to get news once more from civilized lands; he proved to be a lively, chatty man of the world, and a good specimen of western go-ahead-itiveness. He left in the morning for California; and, much to our regret, Mr. L. deemed it important to go with him.

Remained in camp all of the 28th, and, as we forboded, the vicinity of the liquor sta-stions began to tell fearfully upon the men. Out of fifty teamsters, not more than five or six remained sober, the rest exhibiting the various stages of drunkenness; two or three Mexicans, riding about hurry-skurry, lassoing animals, others driving and beating the cattle, without any definable object; and some stretched in the sun, sleeping off the effects of the debauch. I was greatly alarmed, and began to think our revolvers might soon come into requisition, to protect us from our own band. We finally resolved to leave, and make our way through the desert to Carson River, provided Dr. H. would join us, to be of mutual assistance in fording the outlet, reported to be difficult. But, unfortunately, his horses were too much worn down for a forced march, and his driver, a mean, selfish creature, never could bear to make an extra exertion; and when our intentions became known to young Blodget, the representative of Mr. L. in his absence, he entreated us to remain, lest the men should become thoroughly disorganized and unmanageable—so, under the influence of compulsion and persuasion, we staid.

The next day at 2 P. M. the whole train started, intending to traverse the desert in the night. The first ten miles, over a dry, hard, arid soil, brought us (Blodget, Dr. H., and ourselves) to the outlet about four o'clock. A small party of strangers with horses came up, and, in attempting to ford, found the stream full of quicksands, and were almost hopelessly mired. Pretty soon the ox teams arrived, all hands more or less intoxicated, and still drinking—Egan, for some unaccountable reason, remaining behind. Our carriage, with two pair of cattle to it, was started over; but, about two-thirds of the way, the animals mired, and there remained for an hour, with a fair prospect of remaining all night—a man on each side, waist deep, with just sense enough left to beat the oxen over their heads. We have in the company an African, usually quiet and docile, but, under the influence of liquor, sufficiently contrary and headstrong. He had charge of Mrs. Kinney's "kitchen," and, in spite of the efforts of Mr. F. and Dr. H., he plunged the establishment in before the carriage was extricated, and came so near that a collision seemed inevitable. Just as I was preparing to spring *somewhere*, his team fortunately stuck so utterly fast, that all power of motion was gone; and it appeared to me that the whole must be drowned.

Then ensued a scene of shouting, yelling, swearing, from lungs already hoarse from effort,

beggaring all description—it was perfectly de-
moniac. Finally, with the aid of a long chain,
and cattle on the bank, the carriage was drawn
through; and, one after another, the remaining
were got over, detaining us till nine o'clock.
Some of the oxen were dragged out by chains,
like sticks of timber, and a few were hopelessly
mired and lost.

In the mean time the loose cattle came up,
floundered through, and began to spread themselves upon the arid waste in search of food; and
we feared they would never be gathered again,
but the mass of them finally came to the road,
and were collected as we passed along. It
was a bright moonlight, and the plain before
us a vast waste of sand, drifted into little hillocks, around stunted grease wood and carcasses of dead animals. The intoxicated men
made some trouble by occasionally deviating
from the road, particularly the negro, who
insisted upon following the moon, and broke
the stillness of the desert by singing and talking to his team in various unknown tongues.
Morning broke while we were yet fifteen miles
from Carson River; and then, feeling we could

be of no more use in the train, we left it, and drove on at a rapid rate over the hard road.

But what a scene of desolation did the light of day disclose! It was a barren waste, without a tree or a shrub to relieve the eye, except a few stunted sage bushes. The hills with which it was skirted were groups of rocks, charred and blackened by the breath of extinct volcanoes. Animal life there was none: not even a bird of prey ventured a flight over the parched and arid region. The bones of the dead animals of emigrants were plentifully scattered by the way-side, bleaching in the fierce sun. Death alone appeared to be the presiding deity. Yet there was here and there a solitary cactus flower in the sand—they seemed the evidence of a direct influx from heaven, and gave the assurance that there, even there, amidst the desolation, the protection of the Divine hand was over and around us.

The last five miles was a deep sand—the mules sinking fearfully at every step. Mr. F. and Morse walked wearily on; I tried it, but a few rods completely exhausted me, and I was compelled to burden the tired animals, wishing myself etherealized for their benefit. We reached Carson River at 9 A. M. The rest of the train came straggling in all that day and part of the next, so completely worn down that a delay of some days became necessary to recruit.

Our passage up the river occupied four days, the road rough, water poor, and feed not always abundant. The Sierra gradually presented its dark sides as we journeyed on, with an occasional snowy peak; at a nearer approach we found it densely covered with pine timber. The population was thinly scattered along the river, consisting mostly of liquor and trading stations.

On the 4th of July we encamped within two miles of an establishment called Edge Ranch, at the base of the Sierra, where we remained four days in a hot, dusty, disagreeable place; some fine specimens of crytallized quartz, and a curious collection of calcareous coralline rocks, rewarded our rambles in the vicinity of the camp. The water proved to be bad, and the cattle began to sicken and die in large numbers; and the Captain resolved to find more healthy quarters. The train was finally removed into Wassaw Valley, to await the return of Mr. L. from Sacramento.

A more quiet, secluded, lovely spot, the eye of man never rested upon. We are encamped on a pleasant slope, at the foot of the mountains, under a collection of magnificent pine trees, shooting up to the sky cone-shaped, protecting us from the fierce sun by a dense shade. In front this valley stretches for thirty miles, formed on one side by the Sierra, with its clothing of pine, and on the other by a high, rocky hill, at the foot of which sparkles a bright sheet of water, as wide, though not of the length of our own Cayuga. The pasture is most luxuriant, in which we distinguish clover, and the animals are rapidly recruiting.

13

LETTER XVI.

CARSON VALLEY TO CALIFORNIA.

SAN FRANCISCO, July 26, 1853.

WE are now hastening to the close of our adventures: the next steamer will take us home.

We remained in Wassaw Valley until the 19th, when, becoming wearied with inaction, we concluded to leave—our party consisting of Dr. H., in his wagon, Blodget, with Rob and two other horses, and ourselves with the ever-faithful Morse. With light hearts we bade adieu to the members of the train as we slowly passed them; when we came to Egan, he said laughing: "You are not done with me yet—I intend to escort you nearly to the base of the mountains." He was soon seen galloping in front, until he disappeared in the distance.

Our animals were in fine condition for a rapid drive, and speedily emerging from this lovely retreat, we passed Eagle Ranch, and, after rounding a small spur of the mountain, we came to the river; and at this point commences what is commonly known as "Carson Valley"—and surely a more lovely place the sun never shone upon. We found a comparatively thickly settled neighborhood, fine large farms, luxuriant crops, rail fences, and numerous herds of cattle. At a collection of half a dozen buildings—an incipient village—we found Egan, and a good dinner ready for us, ordered by him as a kind of complimentary farewell. This man, with all his faults, has many excellent qualities; we surely have reason to be grateful to him for numerous kind offices. I now recollect an incident which, in a remarkable degree, illustrates his tact in managing the rough and turbulent spirits placed under his control. One day, in camp at the northern end of Salt Lake, while Dr. Coward was dressing his frost-bitten feet, a man near by, vexed by the contumacy of his mule, was swearing at a round rate. Egan turned to us, and, in a loud voice, said: "I s'pose you know the regulations of the camp;

no man is allowed to swear but that man; he does it so easy, that he is appointed to do all the swearing for the train." This came out with a comical twinkle of the eye; we all laughed; the man ceased his profanity, and slunk away.

Bidding adieu to our late captain, who gave us minute directions as to the journey, we next halted a moment some miles farther on, at the station of Col. Keese, so near the base of the mountain as to be within the shade of the noble trees which clothe its sides. His establishment is on a large scale; a great many horses and mules; great herds of cattle; vast fields inclosed with long pine logs; many a petty German potentate might envy him his possession. The proprietor came to the carriage, and insisted on our not passing without partaking of his hopitality, manifesting a heartiness of reception very difficult to resist. But we were compelled to be expeditious, made our excuses, and moved on. In pursuance of a previous invitation, kindly tendered, we spent the first night in the Mormon train, under the charge of Mr. Edwin Woolly, whose acquaintance we had formed at Salt Lake, and were treated with hospitality.

In the morning we were *en route* at an early hour, with the intention of reaching the second summit of the mighty range before us, and moved rapidly on. About ten we reached the mouth of the cañon, from which the river debouches into the valley; and here was a tent, with a table neatly and tastefully supplied with sundry things tempting to tired travelers; but, though a tidy-appearing female was the presiding genius, we made no halt. The cañon at first presented us a smooth road; its bottom about one-fourth of a mile wide, shaded by pine trees; at the sides, the rocks rose up to a fearful height, and surpassed, in rugged grandeur, anything we had yet seen. As we journeyed upwards, the road became rough and lined with rocky boulders, until it exceeded our worst anticipations, and rendered our progress in the last degree toilsome. We struggled on, however, bravely, up, up, over places that, anywhere else, would have been deemed impassable on level ground, reached the summit of this first plateau of the great

Sierra long after the sun had passed the meridian, and stopped at a green spot to refresh our faithful mules.

In a short time we pushed on, over ground nearly level, five or six miles, fording a branch of the river. Directly in front lay another dark, sullen-looking mountain, the summit of which it was our ambition to reach in the day's ride. But in this we were disappointed. The road finally became rough, and diverged partly to the south, the sun sank down to his resting place, and the twilight began to thicken around us as we descended a sharp pitch into a small basin of fresh grass, bounded by a stream. It now became a matter for serious consideration, whether to stop where the animals could be well fed, or run the risk of reaching the summit. There was a fine moon, and I was anxious to go on; but was wisely overruled, as was amply proved the next day.

We picketed our tired servants, and lit up our camp fire on the margin of the creek. A rough party with horses, encamped on the other side, about half a mile from us, looking like bandits—they probably paid us a similar compliment. It was Mr. F.'s turn to stand sentry the first half of the night. He describes the stillness as so painfully solemn, that it would almost have been a relief had it been interrupted by whooping savages. As midnight approached a dark cloud arose, from which there was a single flash; and a single clap of thunder broke the silence, like the booming of a signal gun.

In the morning we were early aroused and on the road, and soon discovered how foolhardy would have been the attempt to surmount the obstacles before us by the light of the moon. When we reached the base of the steep ascent it seemed utterly impossible to make our way up, over the rough pavement of granite boulders. We did, however, by taking off our baggage, doubling teams, and stopping frequently to breathe the mules. The most difficult obstacle was a perfectly flat rock, about half way up, fifteen feet over, the smooth surface lying at an angle of nearly forty-five degrees, upon which the animals could not stand to draw the carriages. We were hours getting over this place.

After reaching the summit we had a rough up and down road for miles, and finally descended into a valley, having a considerable stream, fed by melting snows, and as clear as crystal. To this succeeded another elevation, long and steep, up which we dragged our slow length, and after overcoming it, reached the crowning labors of the day—another steep mountain, covered with snow.

Could we have reached this point in the morning, as intended, while the snow was still hard from the frost of the previous night, the ascent would have been comparatively easy. As it was, the mules sank fearfully at every step, and this last mile of mountains proved to be the longest and most laborious of the whole route. I walked to the top, while the men were expending their utmost strength in aid of the exhausted animals. Here, then, I stood, on Nevada's summit, and had one of those grand views which may suffice for a lifetime. East, west, north, and south presented a boundless panorama—a wilderness of snowy ridges, rocky peaks, and deep cavities. The road continued descending on a spur of the

mountain, on the right of which was a precipitous descent of thousands of feet, to a small
lake, sparkling in the sun; ond on the left was
a tremendous chasm, winding away out of sight
in a labyrinth of gorges. It was evidently just
at the line of perpetual snow; vegetation had
disappeared, except a few stunted cedars; and
the wind was a keen wintry blast.

All things have an end: men and animals,
and carriages reached the same elevated point,
and we were soon descending; now on hard,
bare earth, then on patches of snow, until sunset found us at a small trading post. Here we
spent a dismal night, the cold wind whistling
like a dirge, to our hungry, supperless animals.
It was Morse's watch, and at daybreak he took
the poor creatures to a place further down,
where grass was found, and helped them to
a hasty breakfast.

The next day's ride was a succession of up
and down, as we passed from one spur of the
mountain to another. Just at sunset we reached a station where we intended to stop, but
the men had the aspect of such unmitigated
cut-throats, that we pushed on. This gave

us a night ride up steep ascents, and down
many steeper descents; the road dark from
the thickening pine forest, with a fair prospect
of lodging in the thickest and darkest portion.
At ten o'clock, however, we found ourselves
in front of another station, so coated with
dust that you could not have recognized us,
where we obtained plenty of good cheer for
man and beast. All traces of snow had disappeared, and the temperature was of summer
mildness. The station was owned by a Mr.
Lason, from the western part of our State,
who has his family with him, and everything
about him looks home-like and civilized. The
next morning, at breakfast, he entertained us
with anecdotes of his winter's residence, in
which the grisly bear largely figured.

We continued the descent over dreadfully
dusty roads, the air growing milder and milder,
until we were fairly down the mountain, when
it became unbearably hot. We had, in forty-
eight hours, traversed from the frigid to the
torrid zone. The country was still descending,
but beautiful, the scattered, spreading trees
and grassy surface giving it the aspect of a

continued park. We passed through a rich gold and agricultural region, the ground alternately dug into confused heaps, in search of the precious metal, and covered with the stubble of the recently gathered crops.

But it is no part of my intention to give you a description of California. It is sufficient to say that we laid aside our camp life at Diamond Springs, the first village at which we arrived after leaving the mountains, and that we reached San Francisco in safety last evening, in a steamer from Sacramento.

73212